Cracking the Code
on the Lost Dutchman Mine

How I Uncovered the Truth About the Gold, Maps, and Murder

Jason Fritsch

DEDICATION

This book is dedicated to my wife, Lisa, whose unwavering support made this journey possible; to the treasure seekers who perished in pursuit of their dreams; and to the Apache peoples, including the Tonto, Pinal, and other Western Apache groups, who defended their ancestral lands. May we honor their legacy by learning from the past and embracing the enduring spirit of those who came before us.

ACKNOWLEDGMENTS

I owe my deepest gratitude to Jeanne Lombardo for her extraordinary skill and dedication in helping bring this story to life. Her guidance and expertise were invaluable.

I want to express my deepest thanks to my loving family: Lisa Fritsch, Josslyn Fritsch, Sage Barraza, Bryce Barraza, Kevin Fritsch, Josh Llewelyn, Ismael Cristian Murillo, David Chavez, Daniella Green, Tyler Green, Johnny Ray Martinez, Benjamin Martinez, Steve Gutierrez, Robert Ginsburg, Scott Johnson, and Richard Nieto. Your shared excitement and assistance through every step of this journey have meant everything to me.

Special thanks to my friends, Daniel Harrington, William Danyluk, Ethan Eisner, Daniel Zrike, Dillon Zrike, Anthony Knight, and Shawn Ostapuk, for their constant encouragement, enthusiasm, and belief in this project.

To all my family and friends: Your steadfast support and unwavering confidence in me helped me reach this summit. This book exists because of you.

The Dutch hunting community's generosity in sharing generations of hard-earned knowledge made this journey possible.

I am grateful to Jeff Swensen, Rich Kaszeta, and Bill Incognito for their photographs, and to Frank Augustine for letting me use his map.

Special thanks to Wayne Tuttle for safeguarding us in the Superstition Mountains and for helping preserve the legend alongside Clay Worst, Bob Schoose, Jack San Felice, Larry Hedrick, and Ron Feldman.

Table of Contents

Introduction

The legend of the Lost Dutchman Mine in Arizona's Superstition Mountains has been retold hundreds of times and remains one of the enduring mysteries of Arizona lore. The search for the mine, and for Jacob Waltz's buried cache of gold ore, has been chronicled in historical works by experts like Sims Ely, Tom Kollenborn, James Swanson, Helen Corbin, Robert Sikorsky, and T. E. Glover, among others. It has also sparked endless speculation by treasure seekers and mystery enthusiasts. A quick online search for "Lost Dutchman Mine" yields 810,000 results, while "books on the Lost Dutchman Mine" returns nearly 600,000 links. Countless Facebook groups and YouTube videos, with titles like "The Dutchman's Clues Made Easy" and "Lost Dutchman Goldmine: FOUND," further fuel the legend.

This has led to a mix of serious research, wild theories, and of course, no shortage of fabulists and fraudsters. As for me, I'm not a history buff by any stretch of the imagination, although I do enjoy a well-crafted documentary. I also don't consider myself a "Dutch hunter," someone obsessed with finding the Lost Dutchman Mine. In fact, until late 2022, I had little interest in the legend.

Then one day, my nine-year-old daughter Josslyn asked an innocent question that launched me down the rabbit hole. It happened on our daily commute to her school, traveling east on US 60 out of Mesa. The Superstition Mountains loomed in the distance, a rugged and magnificent mountain range towering nearly 6,000 feet over the Sonoran Desert. Five days a week I would see that spectacular pile of rock. But on this day, when she asked about the big mountain in front of us, I realized that I didn't know much about it.

"Why do they call it the Superstition Mountains?" she asked.

"I don't know," I said. "I imagine it's because weird things happened there. I heard that there's a lost mine there that no one can find."

"Well, tell me about it," she said.

I told her a little about how people sometimes go missing while searching for the Lost Dutchman Mine, shared a few ghost stories, and maybe mentioned one or two UFO sightings in the area. She was intrigued and wanted to know more, so I said I'd do some research and let her know what I found.

That evening, I started a quick search for the Lost Dutchman Mine. After scrolling through a few pages, I came across a documentary series titled *Legend of the Superstition Mountains*. The documentary, which follows a group of men trying to find the Lost Dutchman Mine, was typical of *History Channel* documentaries in that they injected a good amount of fluff and obviously fictional narratives. But in one of the scenes, the hosts, Wayne Tuttle and Frank Augustine, discuss the so-called Peralta Stone Maps and compare the stones to a paper map Augustine had. Though there were a couple discrepancies, the maps were essentially the same. I noticed a couple of the symbols on the paper map and became curious about them. I finished the series and hopped on YouTube, where I randomly picked a video about the Lost Dutchman Mine. This one discussed some of the clues to the whereabouts of the mine.

I became more intrigued with every new detail, and as the mystery grew, so did my curiosity. It was a local legend, but the deeper I looked, the more expansive and compelling it became. I realized this wasn't just a passing interest; it was the start of a new hobby. After reading countless stories of people who went missing or turned up dead, I became determined to solve it. I wasn't motivated by gold alone. I wanted to put an end to the mystery that continues to lure people from around the world to what could be an early grave. And yes, maybe a small part of me was interested in the gold too.

Estimates vary, but hundreds, possibly thousands, of treasure seekers have died or disappeared searching for the Lost Dutchman Mine. Some bodies were found decapitated or riddled with bullets. According to Wikipedia, 9,000 people head into that harsh, unforgiving terrain each year. How many more will die chasing shadows? That was the turning point for me. This mystery needs to be solved. The mine must be found.

I wasn't the typical treasure seeker, driven by dreams of striking it rich. I simply love a good mystery, and this one was extraordinary.

I'm a data analyst and cybersecurity engineer, and I was also a doctoral candidate in data analytics. I've spent a lot of time buried in security logs. When a system is hacked, there's almost always a trail hidden in those logs. Attackers often try to take control remotely, using tactics like bouncing commands through concealed servers or generating random domains to mask their activity. My job is to trace those breadcrumbs, determine how they got in, and help neutralize the threat. It's investigative work at its core, and as I mentioned earlier, I've always enjoyed a good mystery.

To do this kind of work well, you need to think both creatively and logically. It's like solving a puzzle where not all the pieces fit perfectly. The mystery of the Lost Dutchman Mine captivated me for the same reasons I'm drawn to cybersecurity: it's about following clues, making informed guesses, and knowing when to trust your instincts without losing sight of the facts.

A common mistake among Dutch hunters is the urge to force every clue into a single theory, but that approach rarely works. The legend is crowded with noise, misinformation, contradictions, red herrings, and plain bad data. The real challenge is learning to spot the few truly unique clues that actually matter, the ones that do not simply repeat what is already known. The rest must be set aside, and doing so takes patience, discipline, and a willingness to separate myth from evidence.

There are as many maps as there are theories on how to interpret them. To analyze them properly, you need to ask the right questions: Where does this map lead to? Who made it? ... Now I'll do you one better: Why is there a map? These maps weren't designed for the average miner, ranch hand, or cowboy to understand or follow. They are family heirlooms, meant for the creator's family to keep and interpret. Every map was made to guide them to a mine or mining area rich in ore. The key to understanding each map was passed down orally from one family member to the next; there is never a legend or key included with the map. Many of the maps use obfuscation techniques like mislabeling rivers, recognizable landmarks, mountain ranges, or directional indicators. Anyone who found the map without the family's knowledge would inevitably be led astray. This has led many Dutch hunters to believe each map marks a different location. However, I will demonstrate that most of these maps lead to the same place, the Lost Dutchman Mine.

The lost Dutchman himself, Jacob Waltz, once claimed no cowboy or miner would ever find his mine, and he was right. I believe many who've spent their lives searching are too close to the mystery; they need fresh eyes. As someone about as far from a cowboy or miner as you can get (a self-proclaimed nerd), I found myself in the right place at the right time, with just enough luck to piece the clues together. It's counterintuitive, but often those closest to a mystery are farthest from the truth.

What few Dutch hunters realize is that the very people who shaped the Lost Dutchman legend were often entangled in the mystery themselves. For over a century, the search has relied on a handful of "expert" accounts, but peel back the layers, and you'll find these sources routinely mixed invention with observation. Some did it unintentionally, piecing together fragments of hearsay. Others deliberately planted false clues to throw competitors off the trail. Over time, these speculative tales hardened into gospel truth, repeated in books and documentaries as fact. This mythology became its own obstacle. The closer someone was to the original mystery, the more likely they were to propagate its misconceptions. I was able to make connections that others missed by not knowing the "official" narrative.

That's right. I am certain I have found the famed Lost Dutchman Mine! Not only that, but I have also uncovered several other mysteries of the Superstition Mountains. This book will explain how everything is connected.

In researching this book, I applied the same critical thinking and analytical approach I used in my doctoral research. I compared several historical maps tied to the legend, including the Peralta Heart Map, the Profile Map, and Jacob Waltz's original sketch. I then cross-referenced them with satellite imagery from Google Earth. Patterns began to emerge that were too consistent to ignore. Some may see me as just another Dutch hunter drawn in by the promise of treasure, but I ask only that you examine the evidence and consider the logic behind each step.

This book is structured in three parts. The first focuses on solving the maps. The second explores the connection between Adolph Ruth and Abe Reid. The third centers on Travis Tumlinson and the Dutchman's cache. A clear narrative links these elements, following the most logical and evidence-based path.

There will be some Dutch hunters who refuse to question the validity of what they have been told or what they believe wholeheartedly. For some, this legend is like a religion. But for those willing to step back and look at the facts, I believe this book will offer something new.

A WORD ON THE MAPS

There is a wealth of information about the various maps tied to this story. T. E. Glover provides an excellent summary of these maps in his definitive history, *The Lost Dutchman Mine of Jacob Waltz, Part 1: The Golden Dream*. Glover classifies the maps into four categories: the Stone Maps, the Ruth Maps, the Mexican Maps, and a catch-all category for everything else. The latter includes the very basic sketch allegedly created by Jacob Waltz in the week before his death in 1891. For the purposes of this book, we'll focus on the following maps, each of which will be analyzed in more detail in the text. I figured most Dutch hunters would jump between the maps they were studying, so instead of constantly referring back to earlier sections, I ended up repeating certain key facts with each map to keep things clear. **I encourage everyone to follow along with my analysis by downloading Google Earth (or a similar tool) so you can experience each discovery just as I did.**

- The Peralta Heart Map

- The Profile Map

- The Minas del Oro (Goldmines) Map

- El Cerrotero de Los Minas Oro Apacho [sic] Map (The Map of the Apache Gold Mines)/Frank Fish Map

- The J.W. (Jacob Waltz) Map

- Gonzalez Mexican Mine Map

- The Jacob Waltz Doodle Map

- The Holmes Map

- The Stone Maps

The Peralta Heart Map

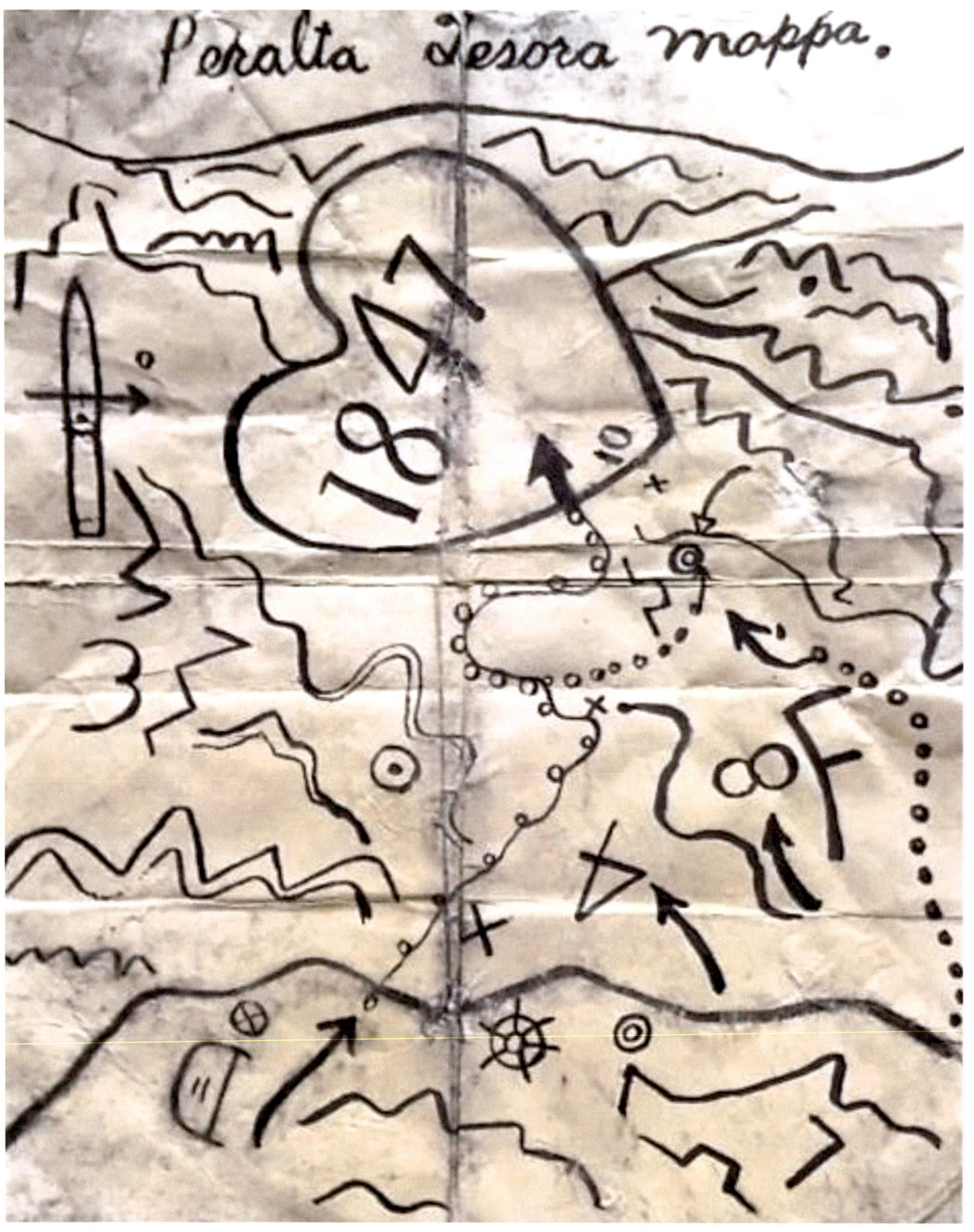

Figure 1- The Peralta Heart Map, courtesy of Frank Augustine

The Peralta Heart Map is a self-referencing map, with the heart symbol at its center representing both the mine and a physical landmark used to identify the correct area. However, this map is intentionally misleading. Even if someone were to discover the heart landmark, they still wouldn't be able to pinpoint the mine's location. The true path to the mine is concealed within symbols and random artifacts; these are the real clues needed to decipher the location.

I was first introduced to this map, along with the Peralta Stone Map, while watching the documentary *Legend of the Superstition Mountains* featuring Frank Augustine and Wayne Tuttle. According to the story, the Peralta Heart Map had been in the possession of Tom Kollenborn, a historian of the Superstition Wilderness and a leading expert on the Lost Dutchman Mine legend. Tom received the map from his late father and later passed it to Augustine. Provenance aside, the moment I overlaid these maps with satellite imagery, patterns emerged that could not be ignored.

The Peralta family, a prominent mining family from Sonora Mexico, has been the subject of much speculation regarding their role in the Lost Dutchman Mine legend. T. E. Glover delves deeply into their history and their connection to the legend in Chapter 6 of his definitive work, *The Lost Dutchman Mine of Jacob Waltz, Part 1: The Golden Dream*. While Glover initially expressed skepticism, his extensive research, based on circumstantial evidence, historical documentation, and genealogical studies of the Peralta family, presents reasonable evidence, if not definitive proof, of a connection between the family and the Lost Dutchman Mine.

My Goonies Moment

A couple of nights after my daughter first asked me about the Superstition Mountains, a suggestion for the six-part History Channel documentary The Lost Dutchman Mine and The Mysteries of the Superstition Mountains popped up in my feed. Although these documentaries sometimes embellish the facts with a bit of fluff and fabrication, I decided to give it a watch. In the TV show, Augustine and Tuttle compare the Peralta Heart Map to the Peralta Stone Map. Augustine mentioned there were subtle differences. It was clear that one was a derivative of the other, but the question remained: which one came first? It seemed like the Stone Maps were derived from the paper Peralta Heart Map, as the paper map contained more detailed information.

After finishing the series, I found another video titled *The Clues of the Dutchman*. The narrator in this video discussed a Board House where the Dutchman had supposedly stayed, located within a five-mile radius of Weaver's Needle. I pulled up Weaver's Needle on Google Maps, calculated the area where the Board House might have been, just north of Queen Valley, and noticed a large flat area along the Peralta Trailhead. And just like that, I saw what, to me, looked like an unmistakable giant heart just outside the circumference (Figure 2).

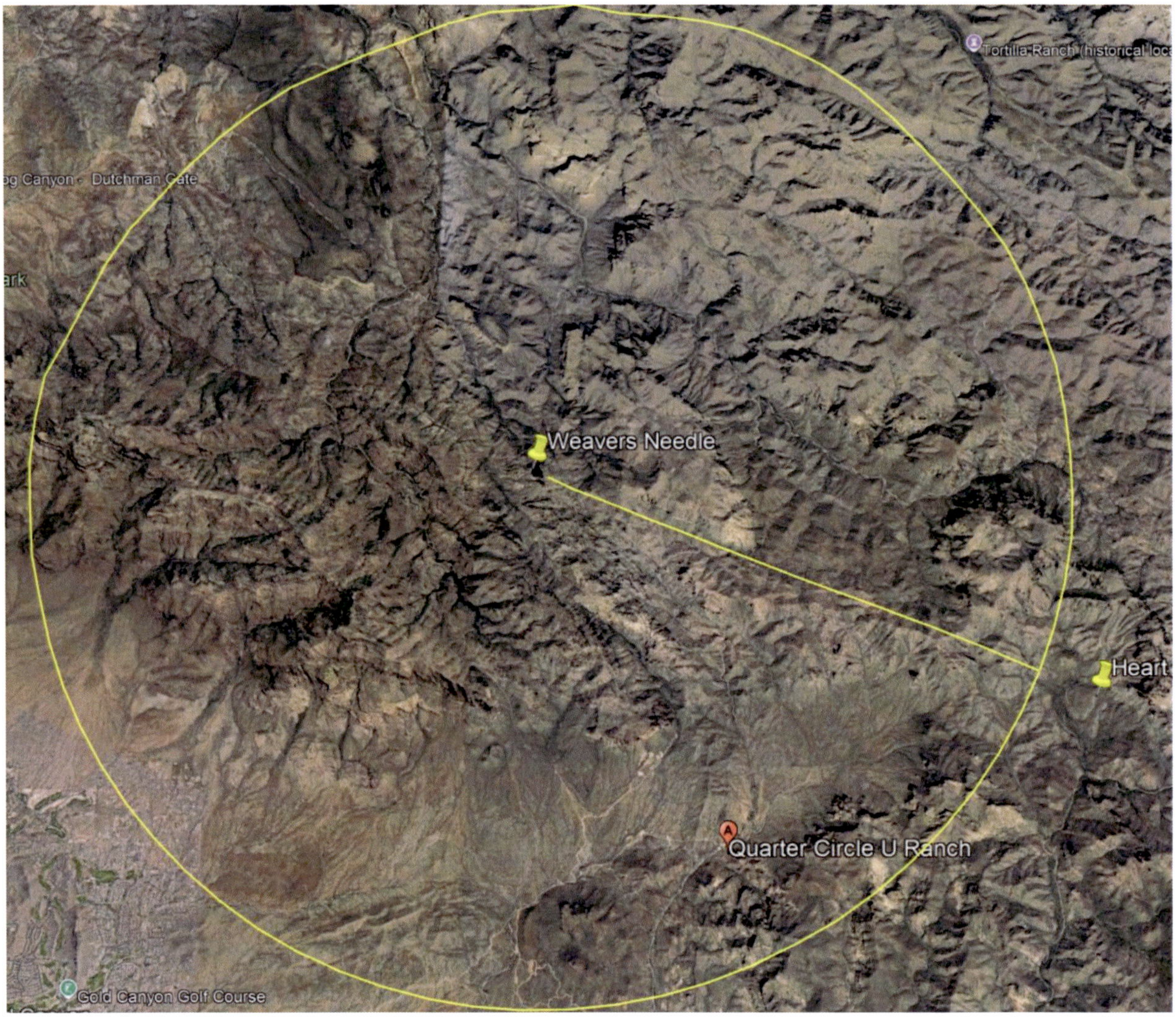

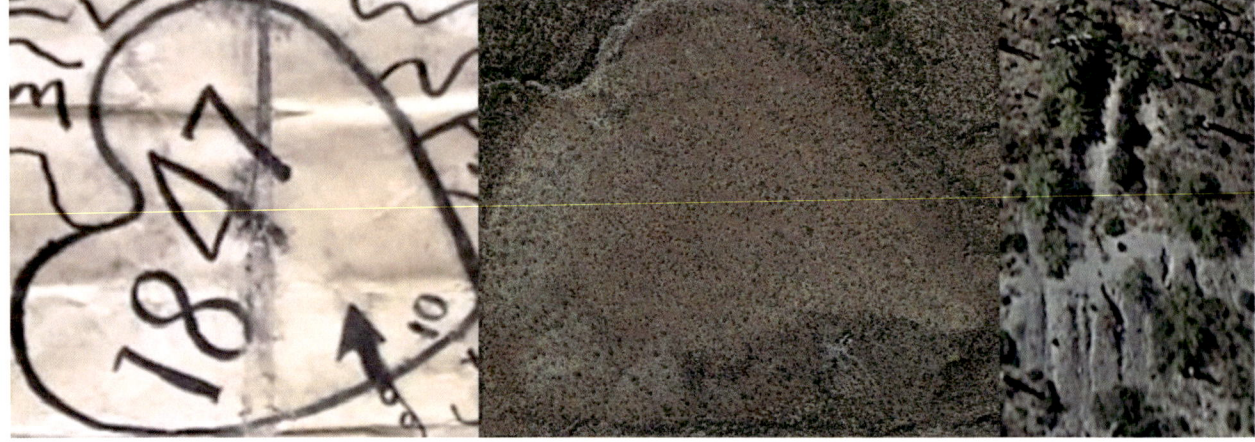

Figure 2- Google Earth Image, five-mile radius from Weaver's Needle

When I compared it to the Peralta Heart Map, the arrow inside the heart pointed directly to the spot where, I would later learn, a prospector named Abe Reid had been digging (Figure 3). At the time, I didn't know much about its history, but Abe Reid was an old-timer who had prospected in the Superstition Mountains for more than twenty years following the Depression. Tom Kollenborn later noted that Reid's efforts left behind a large waste dump, which is still visible today. That was the very spot I had come across while analyzing satellite imagery.

Figure 3-Google Earth image of Abe Reid's Mine location compared to heart on Peralta Heart Map with close-up of dig.

At this point, I thought, this is too easy. What's going on? Why isn't anyone talking about this? So I did some more research and discovered that the area is now called Reid's Water. I typed it in, and a thousand pictures of campers popped up. I figured this must be one of the most searched spots and that everyone had already looked there. But then, I zoomed out, and that's when I saw it. The path leading out of the heart on the default Google Earth map matched the path leading into the heart on the Peralta Heart Map (Figure 4). It hit me then: people had been looking at the map all wrong. Suddenly, everything started to come together. That's when I had my "Goonies" moment. I was about to pinpoint the location of a legendary treasure. But first, more about the map area.

Figure 4- Google Earth image of ravine leading North out of the heart

A Synecdochical Map

Let's take a closer look at both the Google Earth map (Figure 5) and the Peralta Heart Map (Figure 1). Pay attention to the proportions and the physical landmarks. This time, I've highlighted some of the features shown on the Peralta map. The map was likely drawn from a vantage point high on a nearby mountain peak, capturing all the major landmarks. It's clear that I'm not the first person to stumble upon this location; previous excavation attempts are clearly visible. Fortunately for me, those who searched before didn't fully understand how to decipher the map.

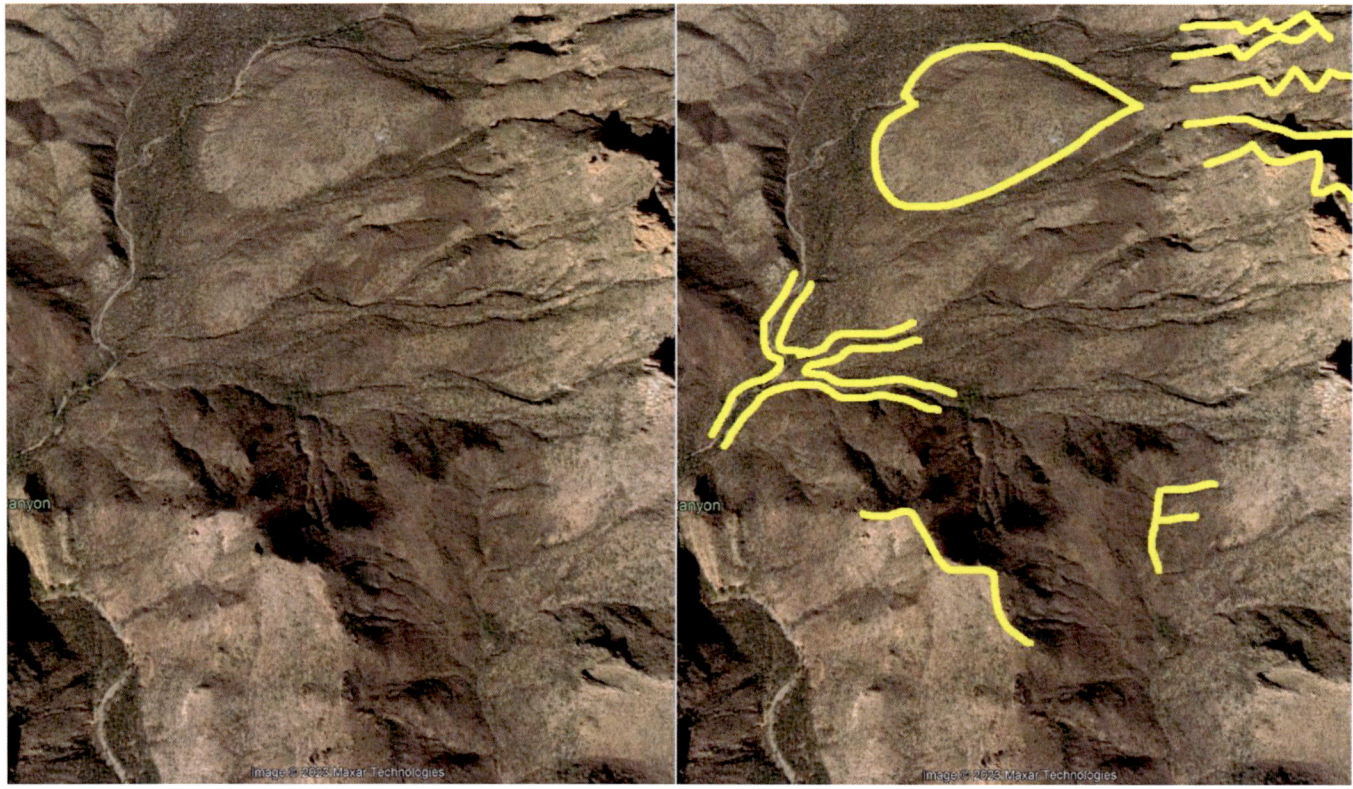

Figure 5- Google Earth image of area depicted in Peralta Heart Map with highlights showing similarities

That's because there's a trick in the old map. The creator didn't just attempt to show a path to the mine; instead, they crafted a synecdochical map, one where a feature stands for something larger or carries deeper significance beyond its literal representation. In this case, it's the heart. The heart on the map can represent both the mine itself and the larger plateau or mesa surrounding it. The heart is not only the location of the mine but also the physical feature, the heart of the mountain, that contains it.

At this point, I was increasingly excited about my new adventure. I was uncovering something that had remained a mystery for hundreds of years. Everything was unfolding right before my eyes. While the heart was the main feature on the map, I noticed several other squiggles, arrows, and symbols scattered throughout. I realized there was more to this map than just locating the heart. That's when I truly gained an appreciation for how powerful Google Earth is. As I examined the different shadows and features on the map, everything clicked into place.

Deciphering the Peralta Heart Map

I began analyzing the other symbols on the Peralta map, starting with the small double circle just below and to the right of the heart's bottom. Initially, I interpreted this double circle as representing the mine. However, as I continued examining the map, I noticed an identical double circle near the bottom (Figure 6).

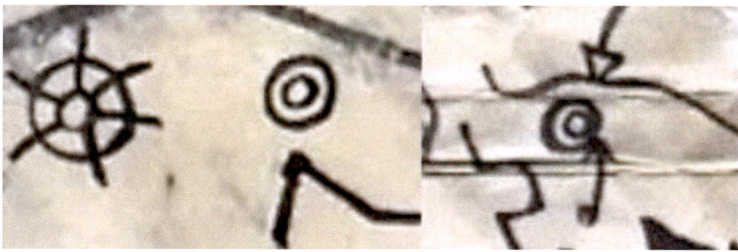

Figure 6- Peralta Heart Map - Double Circles and X

This might suggest there are two mines, but that is not the case. Both circles depict the same mine, shown from different angles. Similarly, the Peralta map includes three Xs: two correspond to specific landmarks, while the third, larger X indicates the journey's starting point beyond the heart (Figure 7a). This will be explained in a later chapter. It's important to remember that throughout this process, the heart serves as the starting point, not the end point. Later, we will explore the significance of the numbers, which are commonly assumed to represent the year 1847.

Figure 7a- Peralta Heart Map - Two Xs on heart map

To decode the Peralta map, start by zooming out in Google Earth to study the surrounding landscape. The heart-shaped landmark serves as the starting point, symbolizing both the mesa's distinctive shape and the mine's location. The Google Earth image below reveals the terrain north of the heart landmark, where a deep ravine traces the path of the trail. Compare this to the route shown on the Peralta map in Figure 8. The trail features eighteen "markers," which indicate distance rather than physical objects. Each marker represents 100 meters. Notice the ravine matches the path drawn on the map. Also note the arrow pointing from the knife on the left side, which points to where the path begins (Figure 7b).

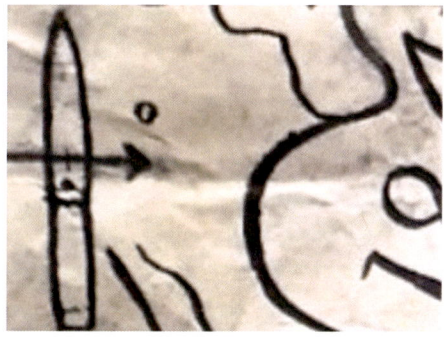

Figure 7b- Knife pointing to starting location

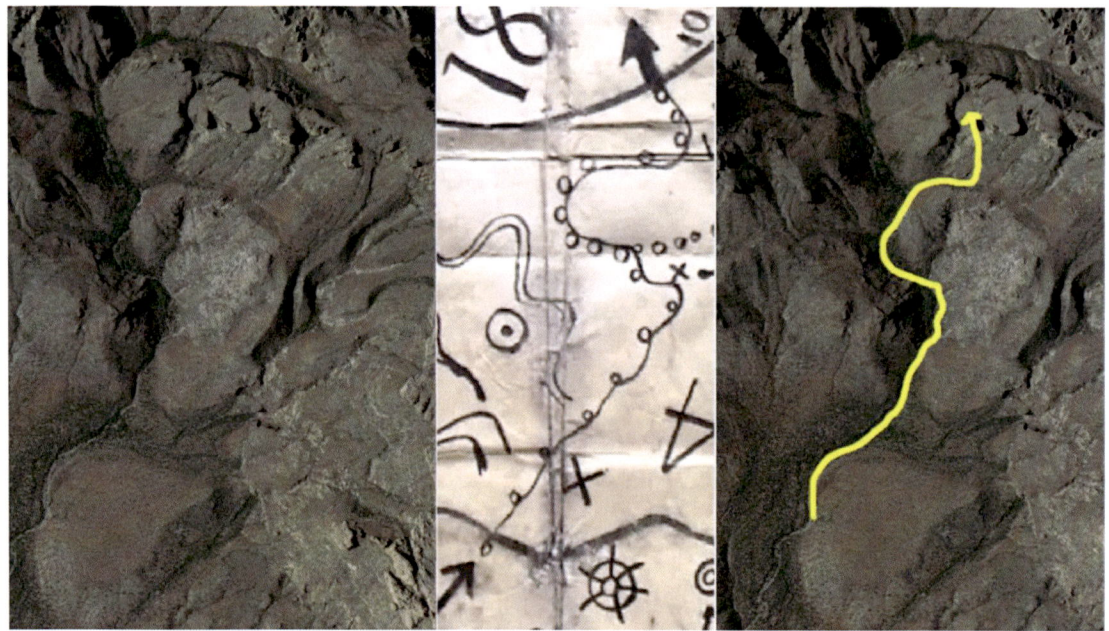

Figure 8- Path on map compared to ravine on Google Earth image

The small X on the Peralta map (Figure 7) represents a physical landmark. This physical landmark is an X-shaped formation, which is visible in the Google Earth maps below and is in the same location on the map (Figure 9).

Figure 9- Google Earth images showing large X formation in same location as depicted on Peralta Heart Map

Not only is the X in these maps exactly where it's indicated on the Peralta map, but it's also a significant landmark on this map, as well as on other maps related to these mines. Now we come to the number inside the heart: 1847. Contrary to what others have surmised, this number does not represent the year. Instead, it indicates the distance, in meters, from the start of the trail (where the knife points) to the mine's entrance (Figure 10).

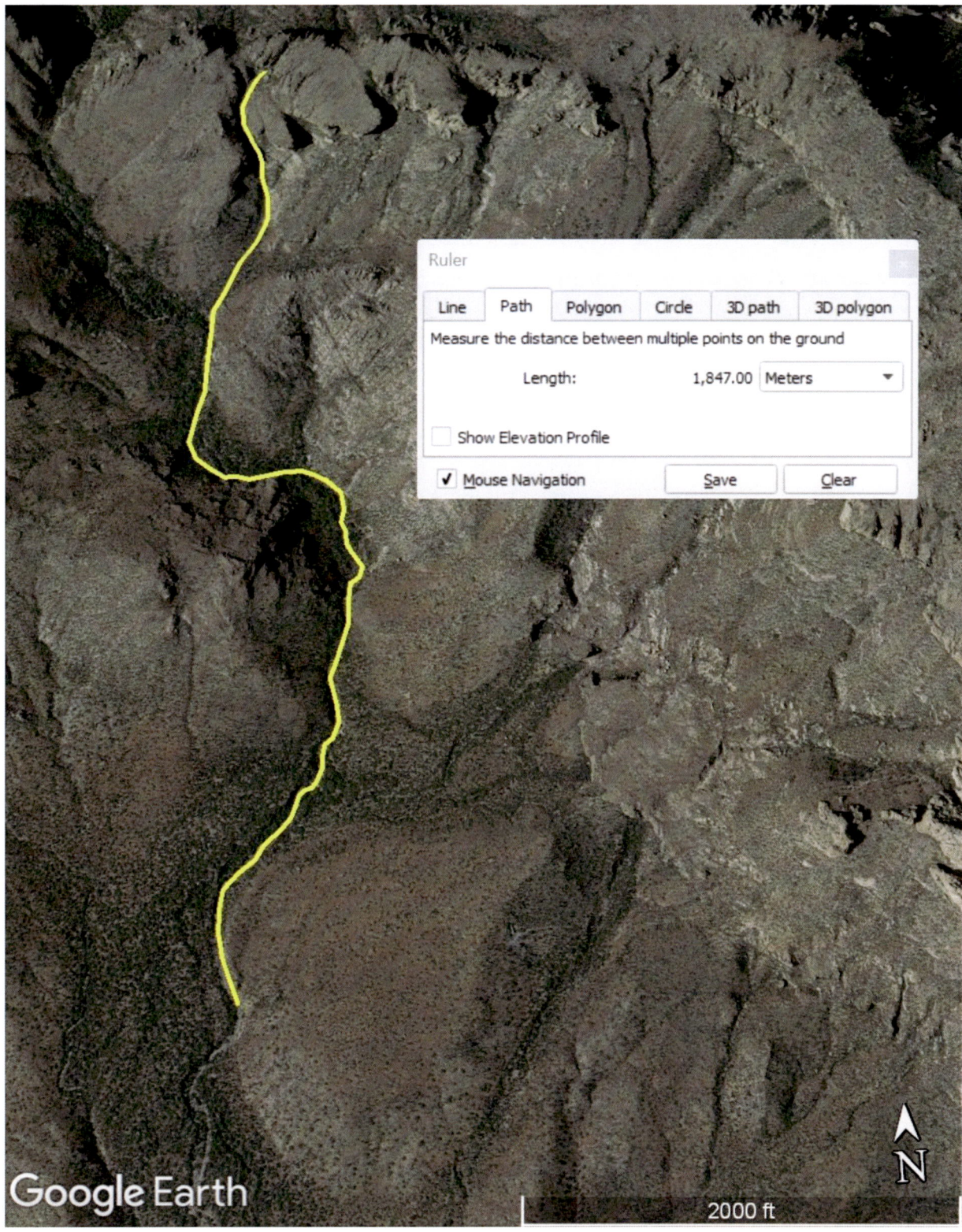

Figure 10- Google Earth image showing exact length of path indicated in Peralta Heart Map where knife points

Calculating the distance wouldn't have been challenging back then; it only required two people and a 100-meter rope. It's worth noting, however, that this route isn't the best way to reach the mine. Jacob Waltz himself often boasted that no one would ever find it. Now we'll discover why.

The Trick in the Trail

Jacob Waltz was quoted saying that no cowboy or miner would ever find his mine. He was very proud of that, but it didn't stop many from trying. The Holmes Manuscript, the only surviving account from any of the early families in Arizona who knew Jacob Waltz, contains a report of an attempt by the author's father to follow the Dutchman to his treasure. Dick Holmes (1865-1930) was a skilled tracker who had worked on the range since childhood. But even he failed, for the Dutchman was a wily protector of his secret, able to detect when he was being followed.

I began to reflect on the significance of Waltz's boast. In roughly 125 years, despite the herculean efforts of experienced cowboys and prospectors, the mine has remained hidden. It made sense to me that a cowboy couldn't find it. No cowboy would dismount, yet reaching the mine demands it. As for miners, no miner would think to go where you need to go. A trick of perspective makes the foothills vanish into the mountain's bulk, like a painter blending foreground and background into one continuous slope. Unless you've been near the mine, there aren't many clues to the mineralization of that area, such as tailings (waste rock), varicolored rock, or quartz.

At any rate, the trail as depicted on maps looks nearly impossible once you're out there, but there is a path. Archimedes once said, "The shortest distance between two points is a straight line," and people often apply this principle figuratively to many areas of life. But for me, the real-life lesson of that principle is that *there is always a path between two points*, even if it's not the shortest. And that leads me to the famed "trick in the trail."

You need to be very fit to follow the path on the maps. I'm not exactly the athletic type myself, more of a hefty Trekkie than a Dutch hunter. My only tan is the permanent one from my computer screen. So, on my first attempt, I brought my nephew and his friend with me. I sent them ahead while I waited at Coffee Flat Canyon. They followed the squiggly path leading up to the arrow in the heart, as indicated on the Peralta map. Now, these two guys are in their early thirties, strong, and they work out. But even they couldn't make it. They were gone the entire day, and when they returned, they were bruised, thirsty, and bloody. The path was simply too arduous, steep, overgrown with thorny brush, and blocked by boulders.

That's when I had my first "aha!" moment. I asked myself, if these two fit young men couldn't traverse that terrain, how could Jacob Waltz have managed it? A weathered old man in his sixties. He certainly wasn't jumping over giant boulders, and neither were his mules. I tried to put myself in the position of this old miner with a mule.

There are countless stories about how the Dutchman first learned of the mine's location. One popular version claims he and a partner had rescued a grandson of the original Peralta patriarch in a game of cards that turned murderous. Miguel Peralta had been stabbed by a crooked card dealer in a small town in Sonora, Mexico, just as Waltz and his partner were passing by. Out of gratitude for saving his life, Miguel told them about the mine and his desire to prospect again. Due to the presence of hostile Apache in the region, and the fact that his father had been killed in a massacre some years earlier, Miguel had stayed away. He was afraid, but now, he saw his chance. He told the two men about the mine and agreed to turn over ownership to them after one last trip. But that's just one story. There are as many origin stories of Jacob Waltz as there are of Batman in the DC Universe.

Now, assuming Waltz used the Peralta map or one very similar, and that he followed the arrow in the heart, there had to be another piece to the puzzle. Waltz gave clues on how to reach his mine, knowing they would mislead anyone searching for it. The *trick in the trail* is somewhat indicated in the map. That's when I realized the arrow did not indicate the location of the mine, but rather the point at which to start the journey. The proper way to follow this map is to enter the heart where the arrow indicates and go north, bypassing the rough ravine (Figure 11 and Figure 13).

Figure 11- Heart from Peralta Heart Map with arrow showing where to enter the heart.

Now, observe the secondary path to the right of the letter "F" (highlighted below). Overlooked by most researchers, this route may be just as critical as the heart's main trail, perhaps even the Dutchman's true approach.

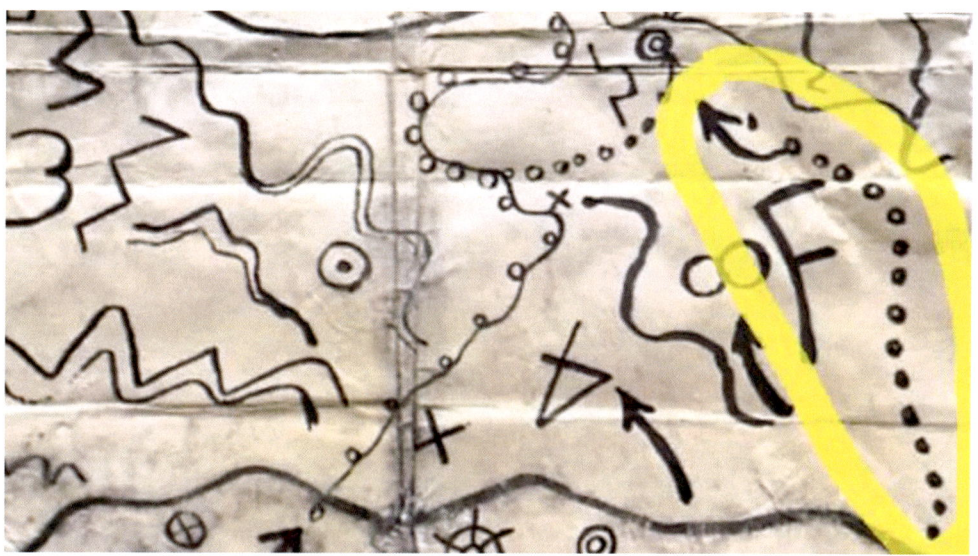

Figure 12- Path to take on heart from where the arrow starts

Now, move that highlighted path over to the heart. This reveals the true path out of the heart.

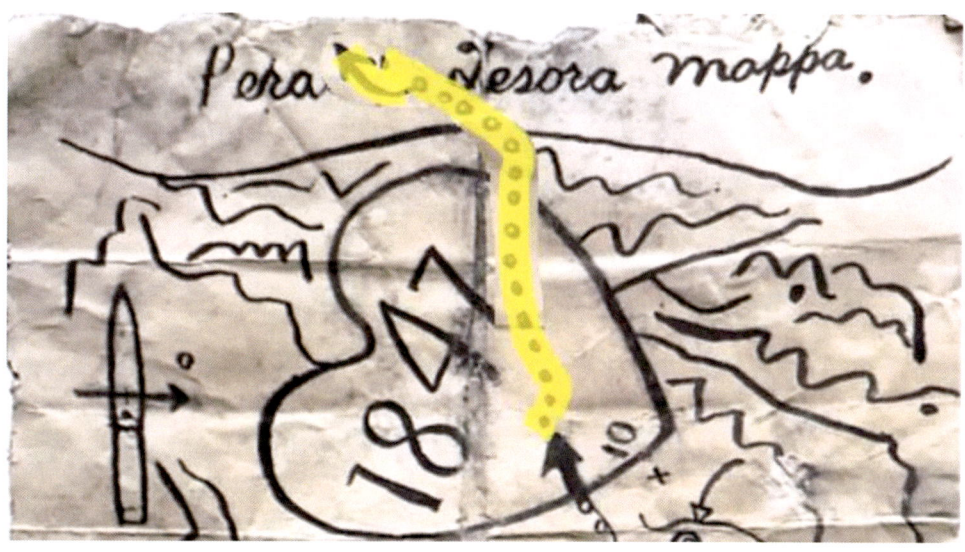

Figure 13- Superimposed image of path over heart

13

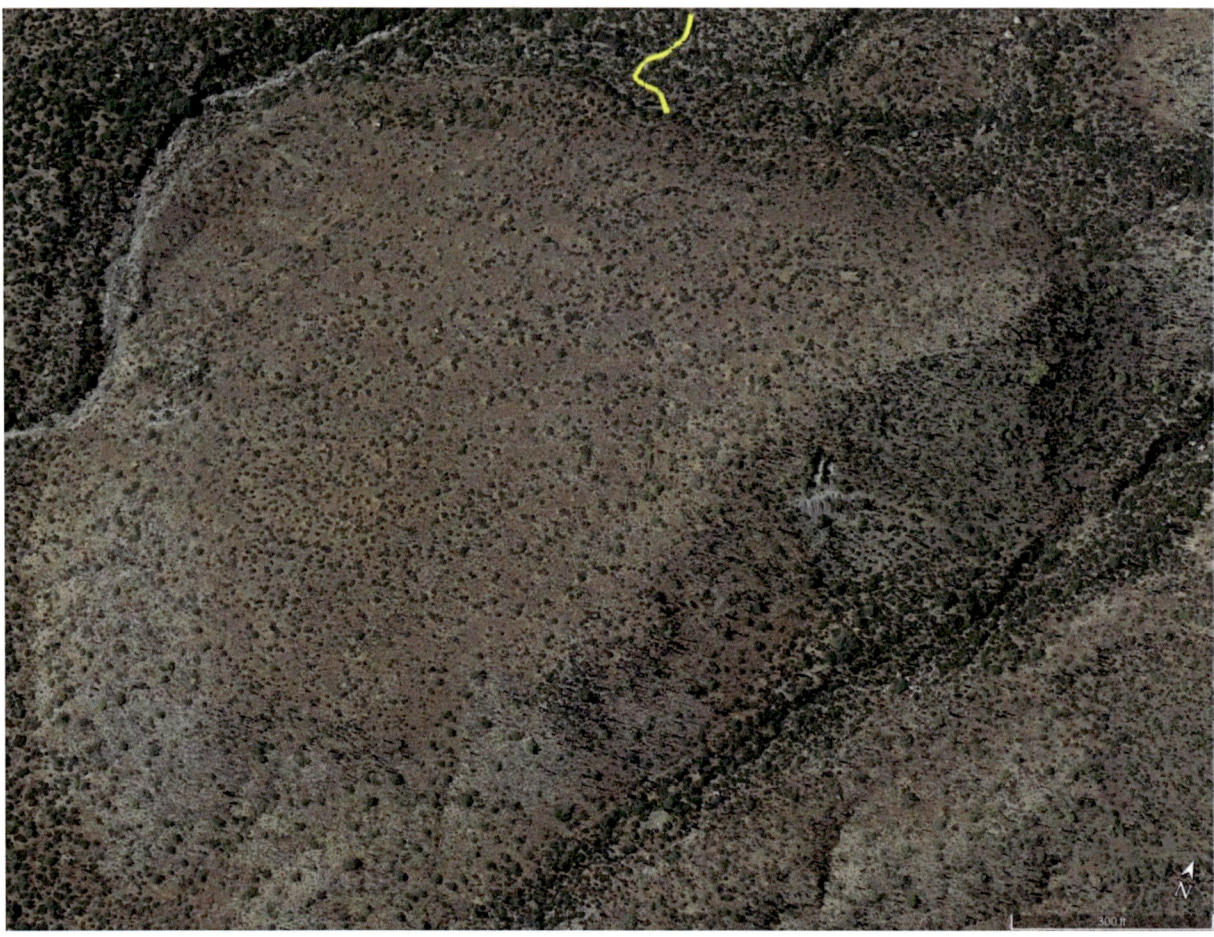

Figure 14- Only path out of the heart, found by using elevation changes in Google Earth

Recall that the assumed path, marked by a line and 18 markers leading to the heart, proved impassable for my nephew and his friend. Convinced there had to be a viable route, I analyzed the area's Google Earth maps, using exaggerated elevation changes to pinpoint the path's exact location (Figure 14). Returning, we discovered it: a narrow, brush-choked footpath, just two- to three-feet-wide, threading through the ravine. Though invisible on satellite imagery, we navigated it successfully. This sole crossing point has become our designated rest stop; we call it "The Bench." The granite slab's flat surface makes perfect seating. The larger X (on the right of Figure 7) also marks this area, approximately 200 meters north. The trick? Follow the game trails through this hidden passage. The animal-shaped symbol at the path's start may represent this very route (Figure 15).

Figure 15- Animal symbol found on Peralta Heart Map

There's no viable route for a hiker with a horse to reach the mine. Solving its location was the easy part; I pinpointed it within hours. But accessing it? That proved far harder. I now faced the real test: reaching it. My next challenge was deciphering the remaining symbols on the Peralta map. What secrets did they hold?

A Five-Mile Radius

Before continuing to decipher the symbols, I revisited what I'd learned about the Dutchman's story. One version holds that Waltz visited the Board House for supplies, located within what is now the Quarter Circle U Ranch at the southern end of the Superstition Mountains. While several locations could fit this account, the Quarter Circle U remains the most probable. The story claims Waltz would complete these supply runs in a single day. Since the exact duration remains unknown. I used an eight-hour window as my baseline. This timeframe suggested the mine must lie within a radius a person and mule could traverse in eight hours over rough terrain. My research indicated it can't be more than five miles, accounting for both the landscape and a laden mule's pace. Just as this theory was forming, I remembered some details from the Adolph Ruth story.

Adolph Ruth was a veterinarian and treasure seeker who was given some maps found in Mexico. He hired some cowboys to pack him into the Superstitions to look for the mine. This was in 1931. He disappeared shortly afterward and, in 1932, turned up dead near Weaver's Needle. They found his skull first with what looked like a bullet hole going through both sides. His body was found about one month later. On his body was a journal with notes about the mine's location from P.C. Bicknell, a famed local prospector and author, as well as the handwritten words *Veni, Vidi, Vici* ("I came, I saw, I conquered"). In other words, Ruth claimed to have found the mine.

The notes he wrote from P.C. Bicknell stated:
"It lies within an imaginary circle whose diameter is not more than five miles and whose center is marked by Weaver's Needle…"
He also mentioned a "monumented trail" in a north-trending canyon. I ignored the portion where it said diameter and changed that to radius for my search, as it makes more sense in describing a location with a center.

Now I had two locations to work with: the Board House and Weaver's Needle. I plotted out a five-mile radius with Weaver's Needle at the center and continued my analysis. There is a chance Adolph Ruth probably found the heart or at least got to Randolph's Canyon using some of the same clues I did. As for whether he was murdered, who can say with certainty? But as we'll see, somebody saw an opportunity and took advantage of his death.

The Shadows

I returned to my maps. This is where the shadows become important. First, let's revisit the details of the Peralta Heart Map. I had already estimated the general area of the mine, but to pinpoint it precisely, you need more clues. Recall the numbers 4 and 7 mentioned earlier. These are key to finding the mine's entrance. Below is the *number 7* clue: the double circle with radiating spokes, which people thought was a medicine wheel or wagon wheel (Figure 16), represents the sun. It means the sun must be positioned to the west of the mine to interpret the other clues.

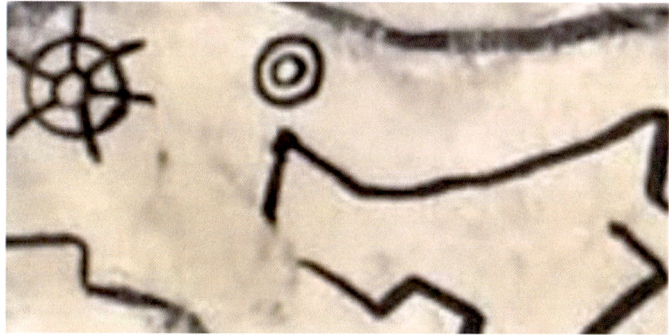

Figure 16- Symbols showing how to read the map - Sun must be in the East

The omega symbol remains one of the most debated symbols and has long puzzled Dutch hunters (Figure 17). What does it represent? Some say it's a pit; others think it's a hill. I came to a different conclusion: it's the shadow of a hill. Both the small downward-pointing arrow and the omega are shadows. The hill casts a shadow shaped like a sombrero, and the Horsehead rockface casts the shadow of the arrow (Figure 18).

Figure 17- Hat/Omega symbol and arrow symbols found on the Peralta Heart Map

Figure 18- Google Earth image showing shadows of that resemble a hat and arrow with the mine between them

The Google Earth map above shows the area indicated in the map (Figure 18). It is easy to see the entrance today.

The mine can be seen between the shadow of the hat and that of the arrow.

The Dutchman's mine is clearly visible northwest of the Mexican mine, which goes all the way through to the other side of the mountain. Remarkably, Google Earth's default 5:00 p.m. view showed the hat-shaped rock and arrow shadows. I'd only been searching for a total of two hours when the location seemed to reveal itself.

Cross-referencing clues from *Mysteries of the Superstition Mountains* confirmed key details: the Mexican mine lies ten feet to the right of the Dutchman's, tunneling completely through (Figure 19). The Dutchman described his mine's entrance as cone-shaped, and there it was on Google Earth. **I measured the distance to this hill from Weaver's Needle, and it was exactly 5 miles**.

Let's look at another Peralta map where shadows are used to hide the truth, the Profile Map.

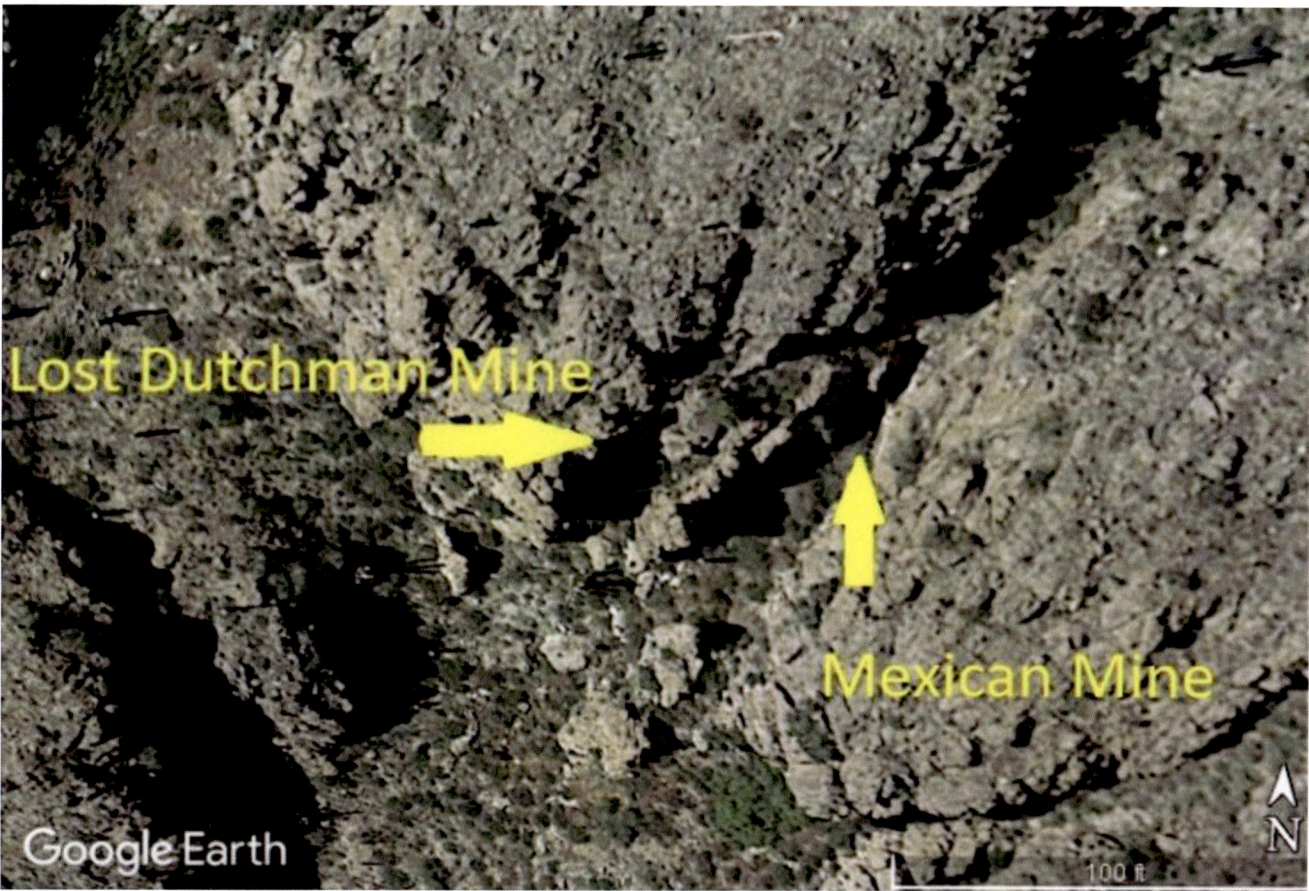

Figure 19- Google Earth image showing the Mexican Mine next to the Lost Dutchman Mine

The Profile Map

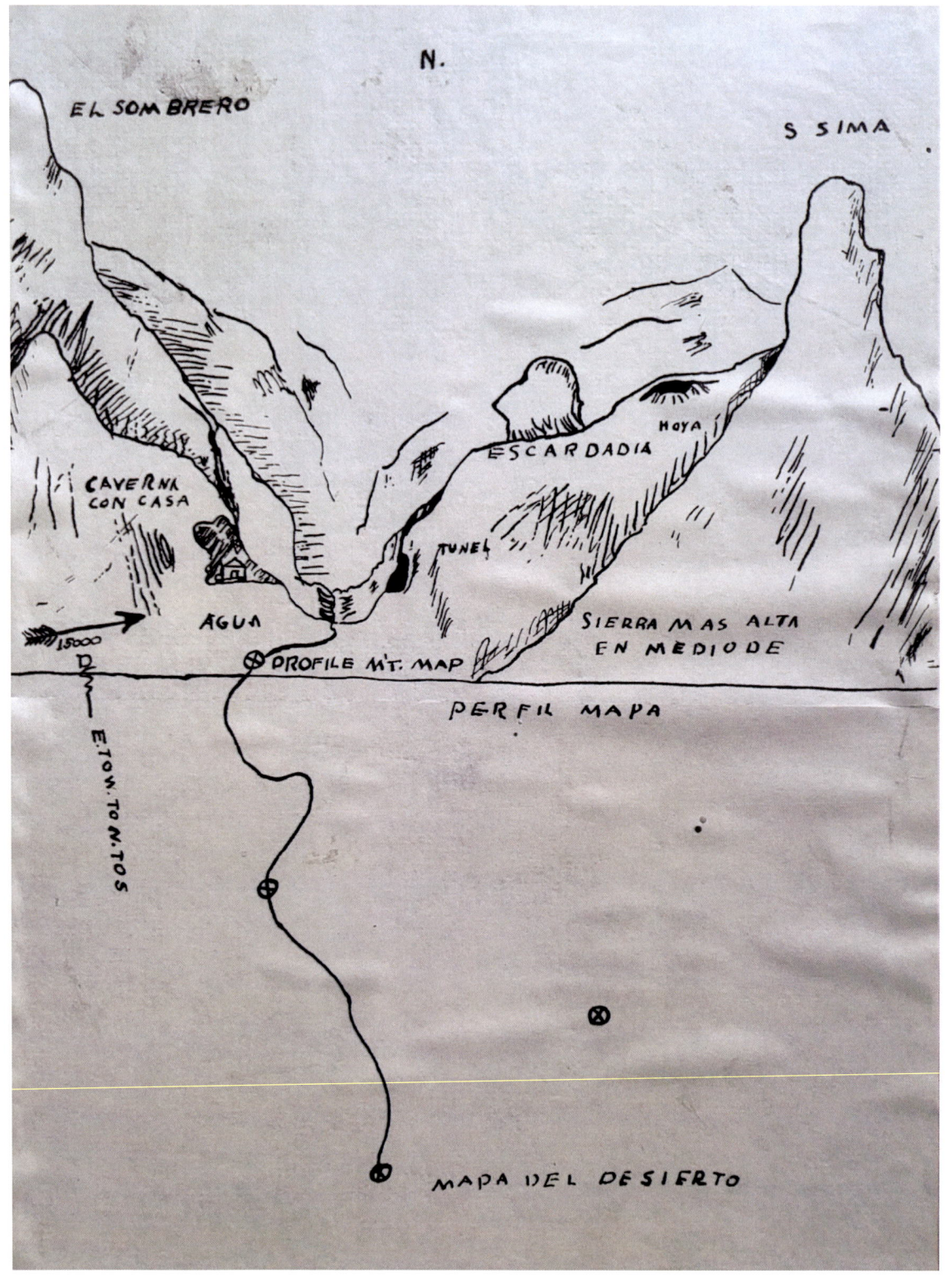

Figure 20- Profile Map

This map is part of a collection of Mexican maps associated with the Peralta family, and there are several versions with small differences. It has sparked considerable debate among those trying to interpret it. One theory holds that the names of the two mountains depicted in the upper portion of the map refer to mountains in New Mexico, where the Peralta family historically lived. While it is true the family did own famous silver mines in what is now New Mexico, I believe they intentionally obscured the actual names of these mountains to hide the true location of their gold mine. To me, this map aligns closely with the Peralta Heart Map.

A key issue arises when attempting to read the map literally. My searches for the name of the mountain on the right, "S. Sima" or "South Sima" in New Mexico, yielded no results. Knowledge of Spanish provides additional evidence that "S. Sima" does not refer to a mountain of that name. In Spanish, the word for "summit" is "cima," and variations of this spelling appear elsewhere on the map. Therefore, I interpret "S. Sima" to mean "the south peak." Additionally, at the base of the mountain, the words "sierra más alta" translate to "the highest mountain range."

The creators of this map introduced yet another layer of obfuscation to the mystery. While "El Sombrero" clearly marks Weaver's Needle on the map, the term simultaneously refers to both the mountain directly north of the mine and occasionally to the heart-shaped mesa. I believe they employed this deliberate ambiguity to further confuse outsiders. Other cartographic irregularities will be examined later, but we must remember these mapmakers were masters of their craft. Mexican and Spanish miners enjoyed global renown, with nations regularly sending their own tradesmen to study under them. As fortune hunters increasingly flooded the region, the Peralta family and others likely developed coded symbols only they could interpret, a calculated effort to conceal their mine's true location.

Now, let's analyze the peak labeled "El Sombrero" on the map's left side. At the base of this formation, along the far, left margin, appear two additional clues: an arrow and the cryptic notation "15000 E. to W. to N. to S." The arrow's orientation suggests the mountain designated as "S. Sima" lies approximately 15° (EbNE) of Weaver's Needle, while the 15,000 number almost certainly refers to the distance (Figure 21).

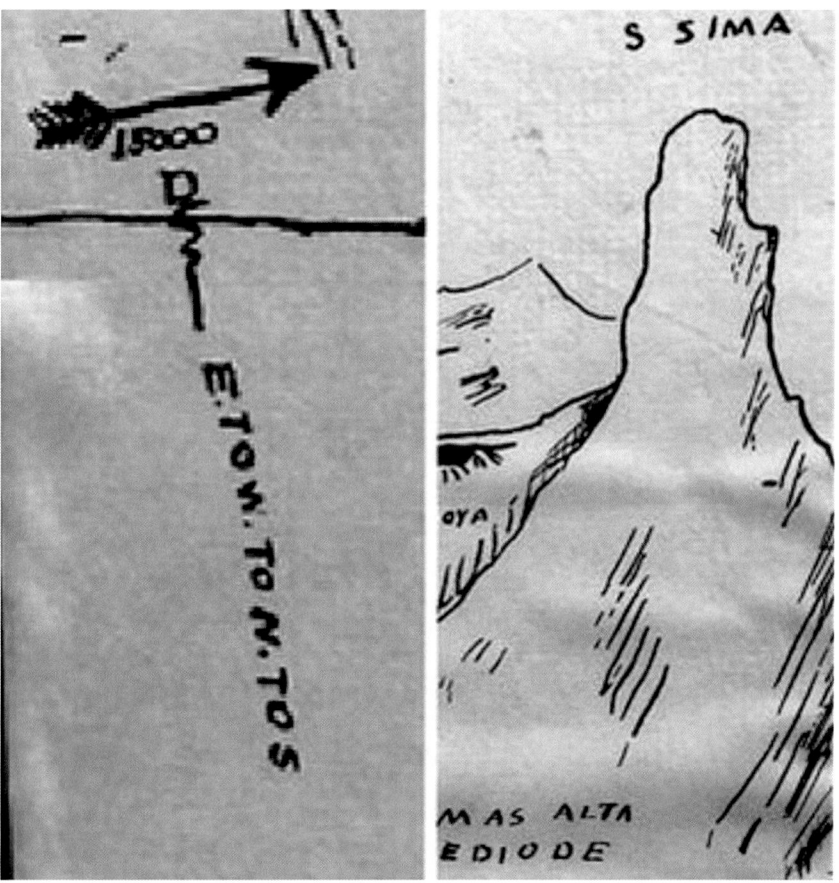

Figure 21- Key features from Profile Map, including an arrow pointing ~15° (EbNE), and S. Sima.

I returned to Google Earth to check if the map matched the satellite images. When I pulled up the region's image, I made an exciting discovery when I followed a 15° vector from Weaver's Needle. I ended up looking at a shadow just south of Roger's Canyon. The image, captured during late-afternoon sunlight, revealed the shadow of a spire, exactly like the shape of S. Sima in the map. Using Google Earth's ruler tool, I measured the distance from Weaver's Needle to this shadow. The measurement came out to exactly 15,000 meters (Figure 22). Once again, I was amazed by how accurate those miners and mapmakers had been.

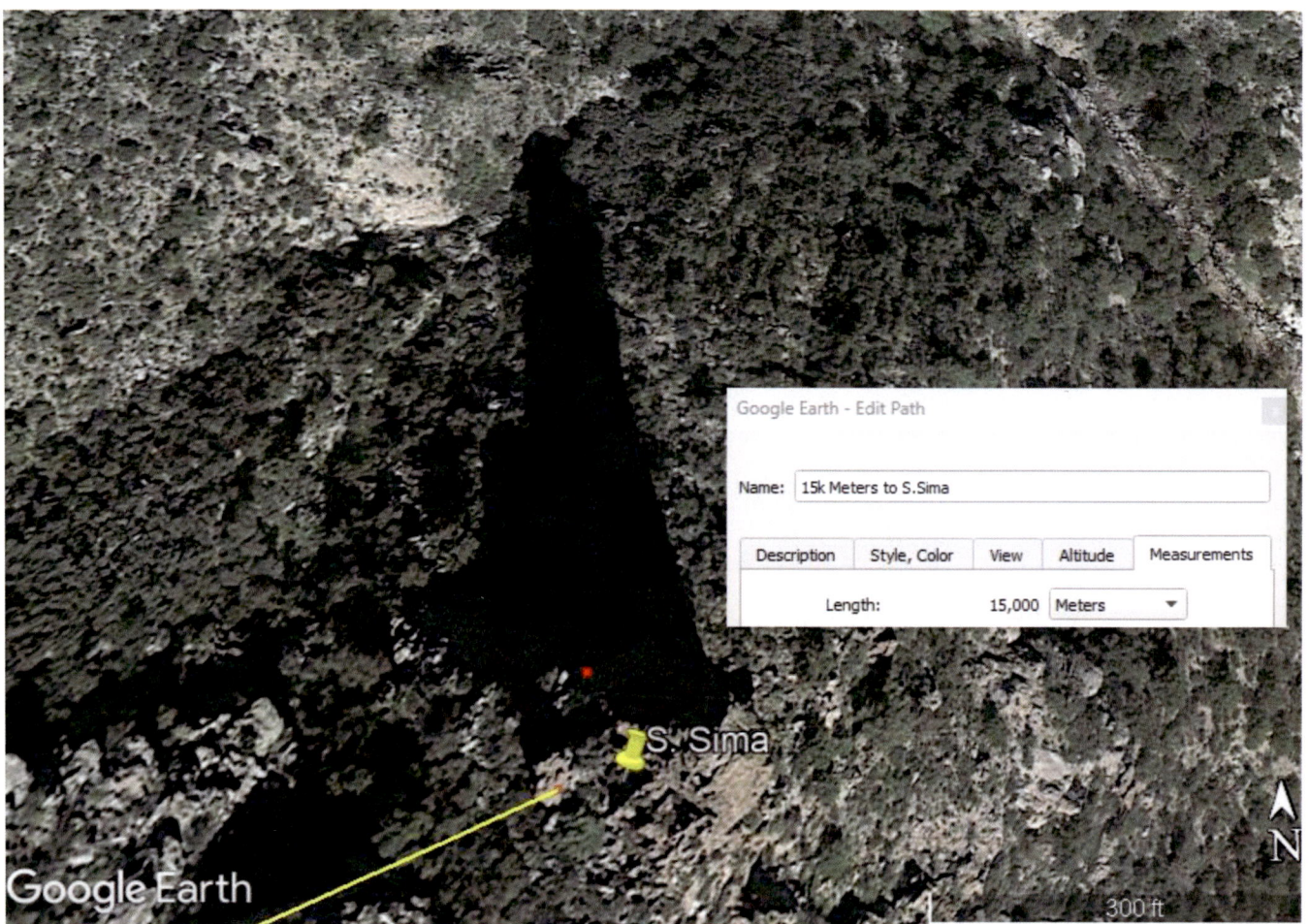

Figure 22- Google Earth image showing shadow cast from S Sima south of Roger's Canyon

Since the directional notation ("E. to W. to N. to S.") was perpendicular to the arrow, I assumed the mine would also lie perpendicular to this line. I expanded the view on Google Earth and measured 7,500 meters from S. Sima along the path I had created toward Weaver's Needle. This placed me directly at the center of that line. Next, I drew a perpendicular line downward, bisecting the 15,000-meter line into two equal parts. From there, I extended a straight line south for 15,000 feet (Figure 23), which led me directly to the mountain summit where both the Dutchman's mine and the Mexican mine are located (Figure 24).

The shadow takes on that distinctive shape only during the evening sun, much like the arrow and omega symbols on the Peralta Heart Map. I've never hiked to Roger's Canyon myself, so I can't speak to the true shape of the spire. Few people post photos of the area, likely out of concern that the ruins might be damaged. If I had to guess, I'd say the actual spire looks very different from what the shadow suggests, adding yet another layer of misdirection to the map. Still, the precision of those early miners and mapmakers never ceases to amaze me. They were cunning, creative, and truly brilliant. They crafted a map so cleverly deceptive that it fooled even the most seasoned experts.

Figure 23- Google Earth image showing both lines

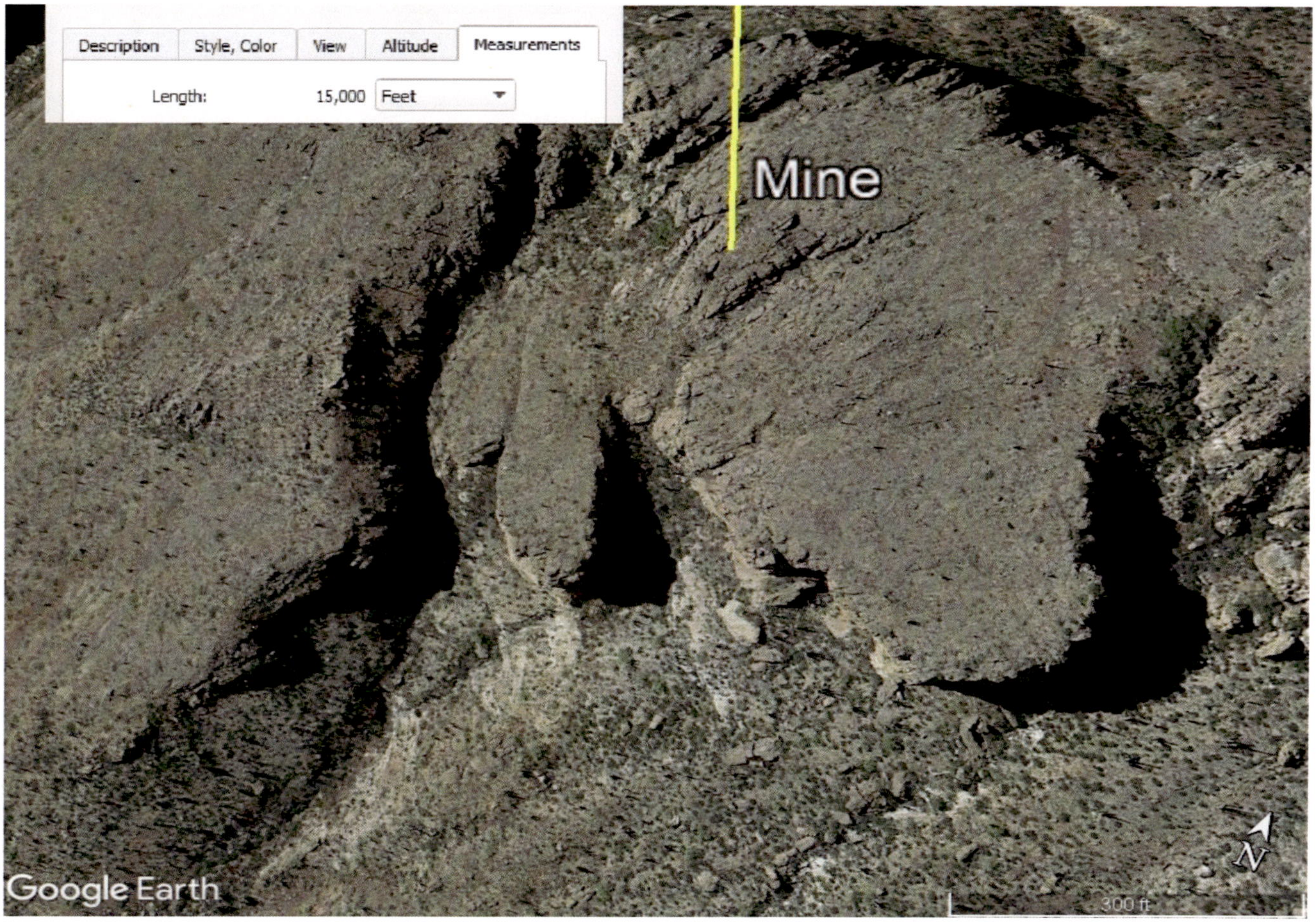

Figure 24- Google Earth image showing where the 15,000, foot bifurcated line ends

Now, I examined the other features depicting this site on the two maps. The trail leading up from the lower portion of the Profile Map matched perfectly with the one on the Peralta Heart Map (Figure 25).

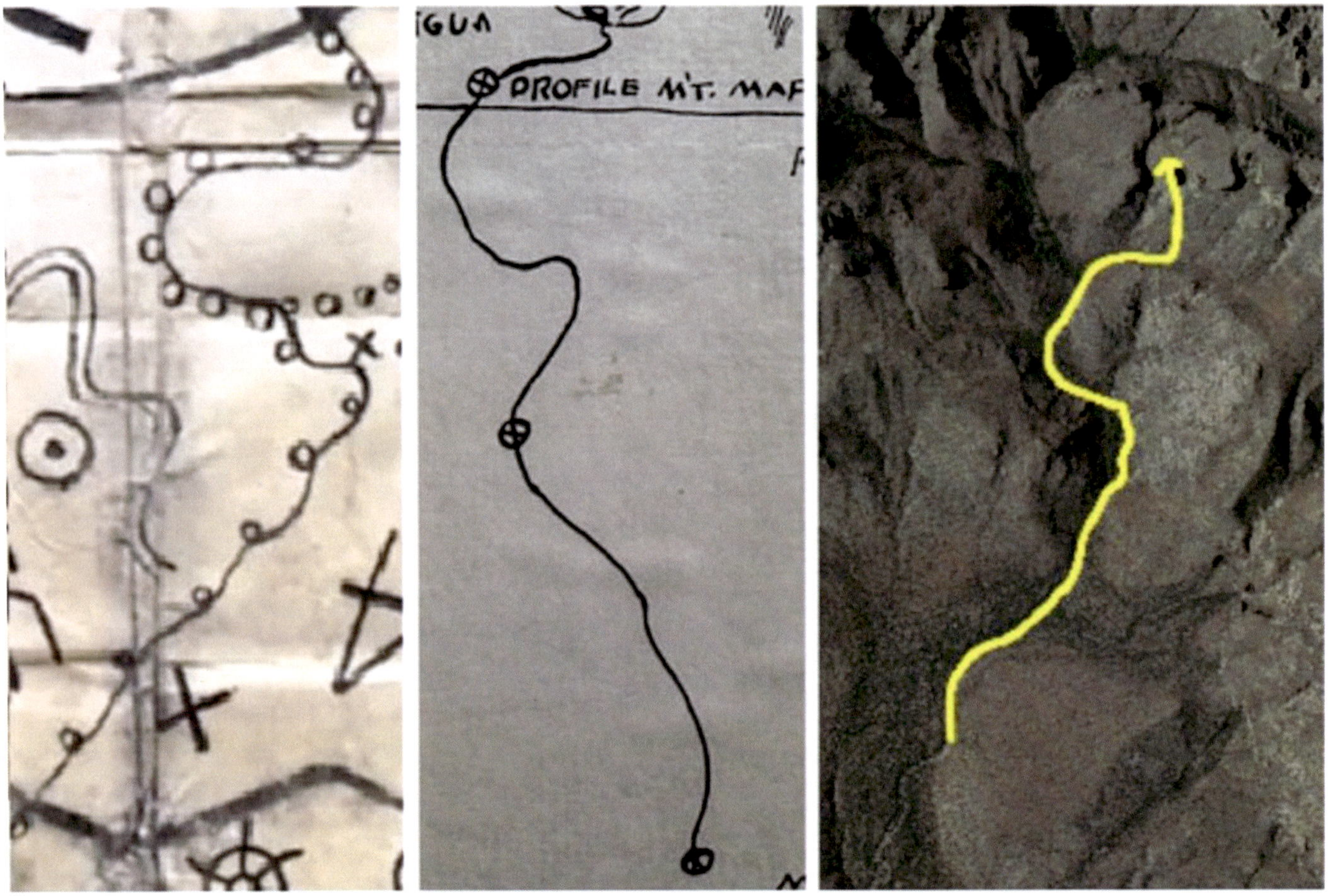

Figure 25- Maps and Google Earth image showing same path

The heart and Xs appear on the map, but there's a trick to uncovering them (Figure 26). You must fold the map along the middle and hold it up to the light to reveal the superimposed X pattern (Figure 29). The boulder depicted on the map represents a large boulder. This boulder is a prominent landmark, measuring over 15 feet in width (Figure 27 and Figure 28). There is one path that can take you to the mine, and it passes by this boulder.

Figure 26- Google Earth image and Xs from Profile Map

Figure 27- Large boulder found on path and image of drawn boulder on Profile Map

Figure 28- Google Earth image showing large boulder on path to the mine below the X formation on top

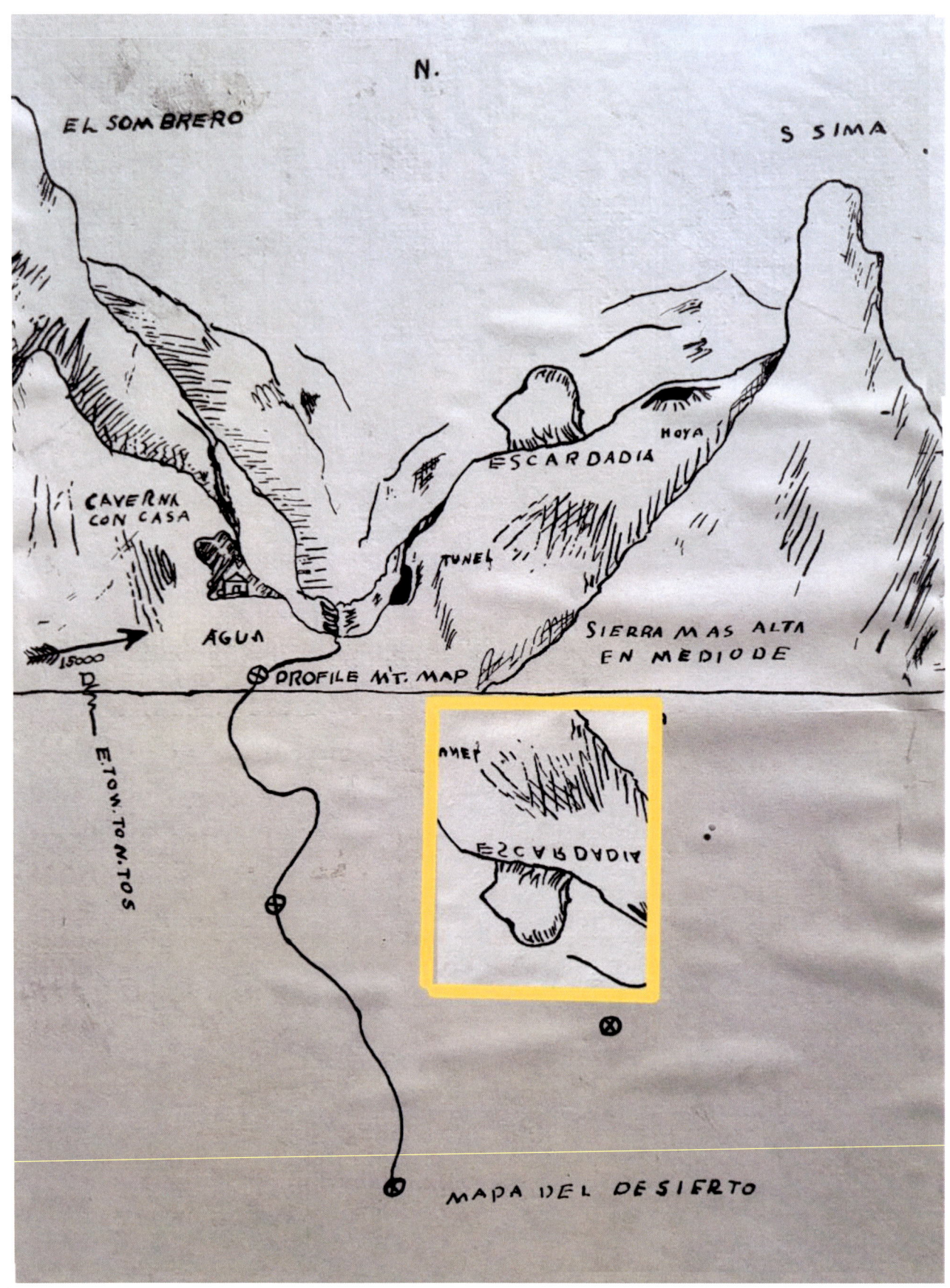

Figure 29- Profile Map with boulder and X's inverted to show on map as heart

Figure 30- (left)Profile Map two-room cave and (right) Cliff Dwellings (Roger's Canyon) by kaszeta (Flickr), used with permission.

The original mapmakers devised a brilliant system of decoys that has misled even the most seasoned Dutchman hunters for generations. Their cleverest trick was using the well-known Roger's Canyon Cliff Dwelling as a lure. They boldly labeled it "Caverna con Casa" (Figure 30) and added an arrow pointing toward the canyon. They even drew the trail to mimic the ravine near Roger's Canyon.

Their trickery mirrors the Peralta Heart Map's successful deception, which misled Abe Reid to dig for decades in the wrong location at the heart-shaped mesa. The fact that these centuries-old tricks continue to misdirect modern treasure hunters stands as testament to their creators' profound understanding of human nature and mastery of deception. It was a honeypot in plain sight, designed to draw attention while quietly leading searchers away from the truth.

Before examining other relevant historical maps, we must address an authenticity question regarding the Profile Map's language. While most notations appear in Spanish, several English markings stand out. The directional instructions "E. to W. to N. to S." clearly use English abbreviations, the Spanish equivalents would be "E. a O. a N. a S." (since "oeste" is Spanish for "west"). Similarly, the word "to" itself is English rather than the Spanish "a." The most telling example appears along the central dividing line: "Perfil Mapa" (Spanish) appears below its English translation, "Profile Mt. Map." This linguistic mixing strongly suggests we're examining a copied version of the original, with later annotations or translations added.

A reasonable question concerns my use of both metric and imperial units when calculating the mine's location, rather than older units like the Spanish "vara," "paso," or "pie." These traditional Spanish measurements often varied depending on the surveyor, whereas standardized metric and imperial units proved far more reliable. Both systems were in widespread use during the 19th century, particularly in mining regions. Spanish, Mexican, French, and German miners typically worked in meters, especially after Mexico officially adopted the metric system in 1857 and fully enforced it by 1896. Meanwhile, English-speaking American prospectors relied on feet and miles, as the U.S. retained its customary units despite legalizing metric alongside them in 1866. Given this clash of measurement systems among treasure hunters, original maps likely existed in multiple versions, some marked in metric, others in imperial. In rare cases, a map might still reference the Spanish "vara," a lingering relic of the colonial era.

The mapmakers relied on permanent landmarks as reference points, making the mine identifiable under any measurement system. Their real brilliance lay in limiting the decryption key to select individuals. By blending metric and imperial units, they created a lasting mystery that kept the mine's location hidden for generations. Few would think to cross-reference both systems, which ensured secrecy that endured over time.

The "Goldmines Map"

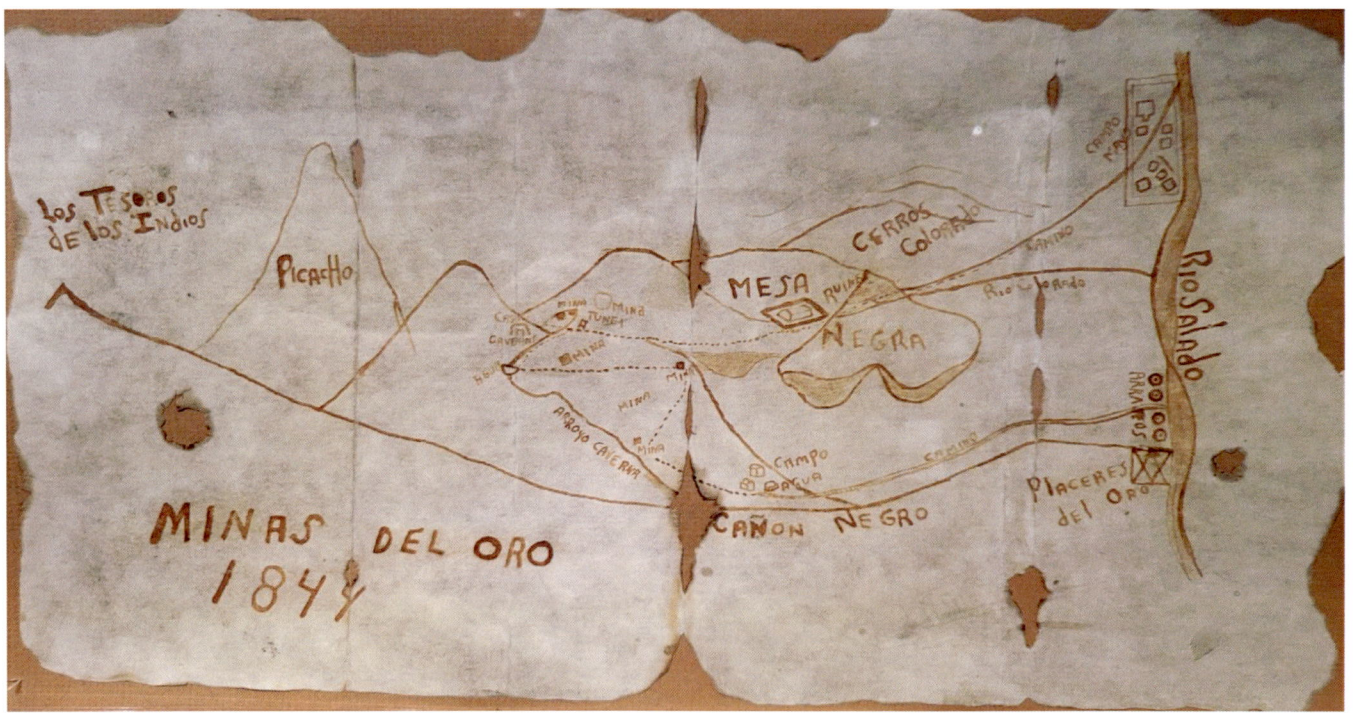

Figure 33- Minas Del Oro (Goldmines Map)

Another of the Mexican maps, known as the "Goldmines Map," is easier to decipher. The heart, located at the center-right and labeled "Mesa Negra" (Black Mesa), stands out prominently, and various paths leading to different mines are clearly outlined (Figure 33). The names of the mountains, as well as the location of the Rio Salado River, have been altered to obscure the true location. However, there is indeed a mesa called Black Mesa in the Superstition Mountains, situated about nine miles northwest of the mine. It's a well-known area and frequently serves as the starting point for many Dutch hunters' searches.

In many of these maps, the Peralta family deliberately switched the names of rivers and canyons to mislead treasure seekers. The map not only shows the mine's location but also indicates other mines the Mexican miners worked through to access the ore. The number "1844" appears on the map, which many have mistakenly interpreted as the year the map was created. However, as with the Peralta Heart Map, the number represents the distance of the path in meters, not a date. The mapmaker employed the same technique used in other Peralta maps, a distance-based reference cleverly hiding the truth for those who weren't meant to find it. Why would someone put a date on a map to a hidden mine, except to deceive or to provide instruction.

There appears to be two paths (the dotted lines), one coming from the east over the heart, and the other following the ravine below the heart (Figure 34). The distance for both paths is roughly 1,844 meters. The direct path over the heart begins just east of the heart, while the southern path starts just below it. It follows the ravine through the area where the other mines are located. This suggests two possible routes, each with similar lengths but different terrain considerations.

Figure 34- Minas Del Oro map showing heart and path

The map also highlights the ruins located just outside the left side of the heart (Figure 34) as well as the *casa caverna* (house cave) on the far left, directly across from the entrance to the mine (Figure 35).

Figure 35- Zoomed-in map showing mines and location of the two-room cave

El Cerrotero de los Minas Oro Apacho Map

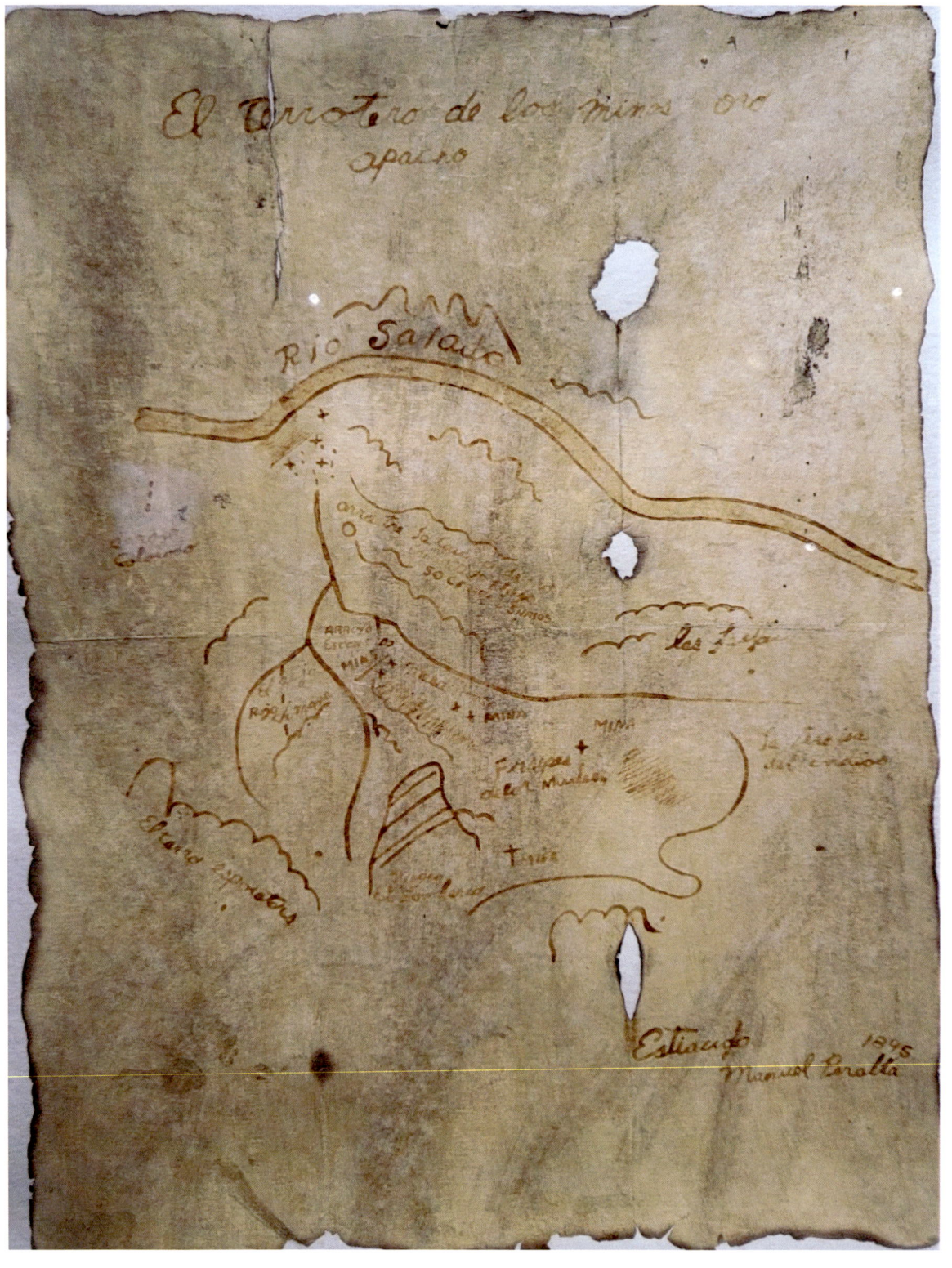

Figure 36- El Cerrotero De Los Minas Oro Apacho Map/ AKA Frank-Fish Map

This is one of the oldest authenticated Peralta maps. It was associated with the famed treasure hunter Frank Fish, who died under mysterious circumstances. There are several versions of this map floating around with different names and labels of the features. The creators employed similar techniques found in other Peralta Maps to obfuscate the true location of the mine. For example, they labeled the ravine north of the mine as the Rio Salado River. The map outlines a path that closely mirrors those in the previous maps we've examined. In my opinion, this map was likely drawn from memory by someone who had visited the mine, as certain features are present but distorted. For instance, the path to the mine is inverted, suggesting that the creator either remembered the general layout but drew it backward or intended for the map to be folded or viewed from behind, possibly through a light source (Figure 37).

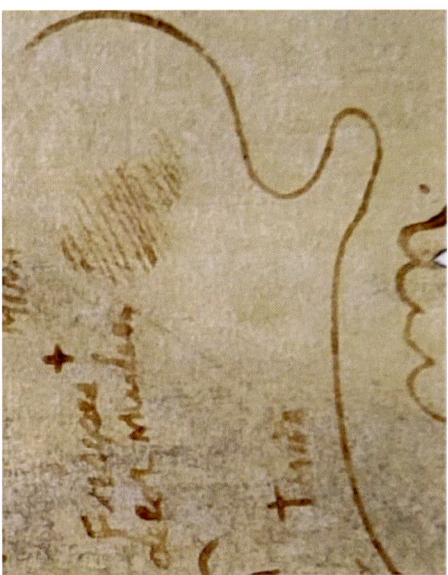

Figure 37- Path of ravine, like the paths in the other maps but backwards

The next image shows the peak at Randolph Canyon. Like other maps that reuse names, this peak is labeled "El Sombrero" (Figure 38). Some maps refer to the heart as the sombrero, while others apply the name to a nearby peak. One map even identifies Weaver's Needle as El Sombrero. The creators used these naming inconsistencies to add another layer of deception, only those intended to understand would recognize the true meaning.

Figure 38- Shape found in map that is likely supposed to represent the peak at Randolph's Canyon.

The peak labeled "El Sombrero" on the map was likely drawn from memory, as its slope faces the opposite direction. This can also suggest that the creator may have intended the map to be folded, aligning the path and peak into their correct positions.

Figure 39a depicts the Xs next to the mine. In this map, the Xs are shown above the mine, though still adjacent. This is another example of the map being drawn from memory. The map also illustrates the three washes next to the Sombrero/Heart (Figure 40).

Figure 39a- Xs shown in map marking same X-shaped landmark as Xs in the other maps

Figure 39b- Area depicted in map (see Figure 40)

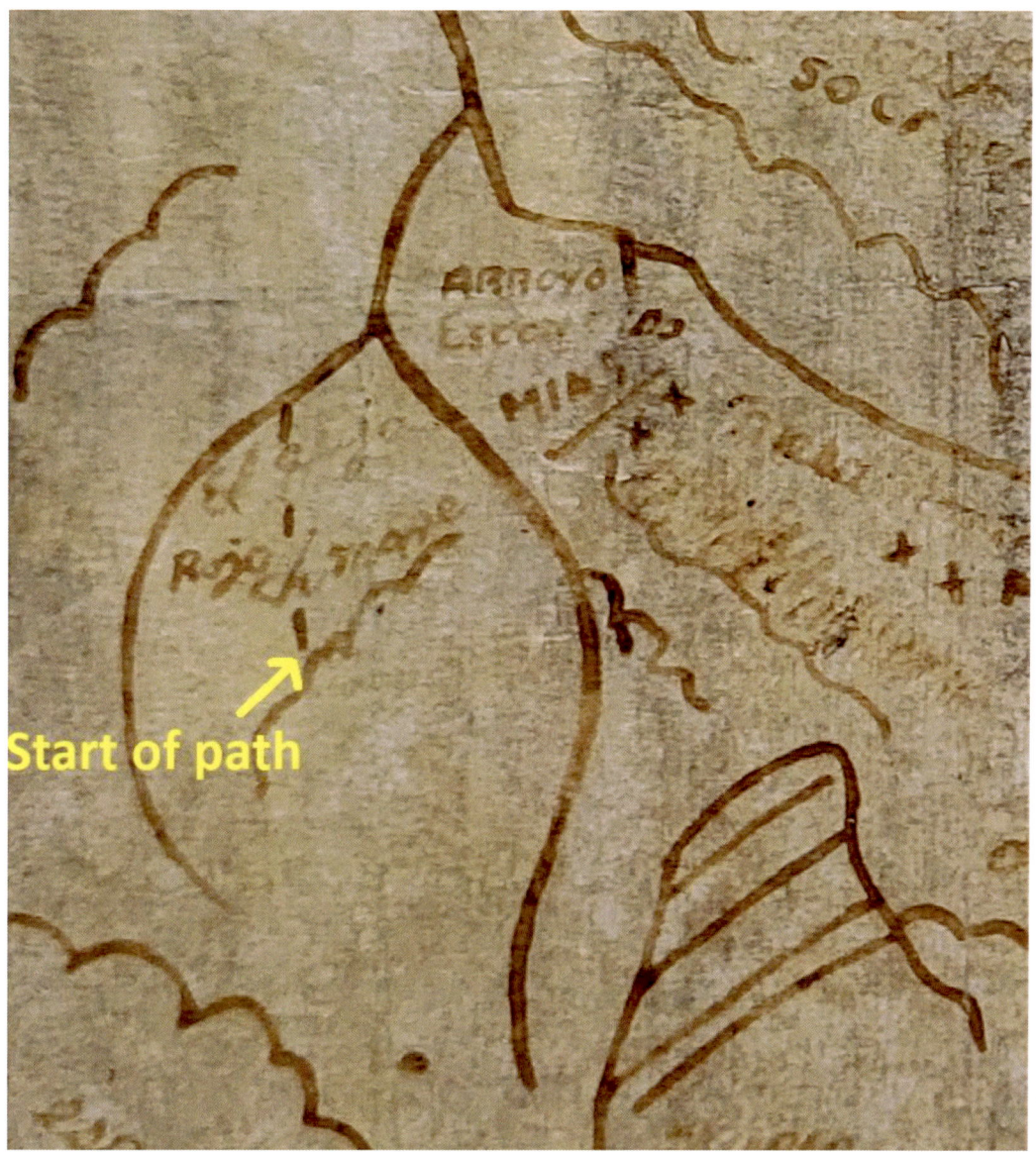

Figure 40- Start of path leading north bypassing a portion of the ravine through the heart mesa towards the Xs.

The writing varies significantly between different versions of this map. Many words are illegible, but fortunately, some key terms stand out clearly enough to be identified. Among them are references to red ("rojo") and hints of a shortcut, most notably the phrase "el corte" (the cut). All versions place these markings in the same critical location: the heart-shaped mesa (Figure 39b). Despite differences in the written labels, each map shows a starting route; follow the dashed line north while bypassing a specific ravine section (Start of path in Figure 40).

Some of the faded and illegible writing likely served as a personal guide for the map's intended owners. These annotations may have helped them recognize specific landmarks and features known only to the map's creator and their trusted family. Each word likely carried a coded meaning, intelligible only to a select few.

Every version of this map includes the number 1845, which is clearly different from the 1847 found on the Peralta Heart Map. These numbers almost certainly refer to measured distances in meters, not dates. They were likely intended to guide searchers close to the mine's location. The repeated use of similar four-digit numbers on both maps suggests a deliberate system for marking distances while hiding important details. Interpreting them as dates makes little sense. Why would someone put a date on a coded treasure map? When viewed as encrypted distance markers, their purpose becomes clear only to those who understand the mapmakers' secret system.

The J. W. Map

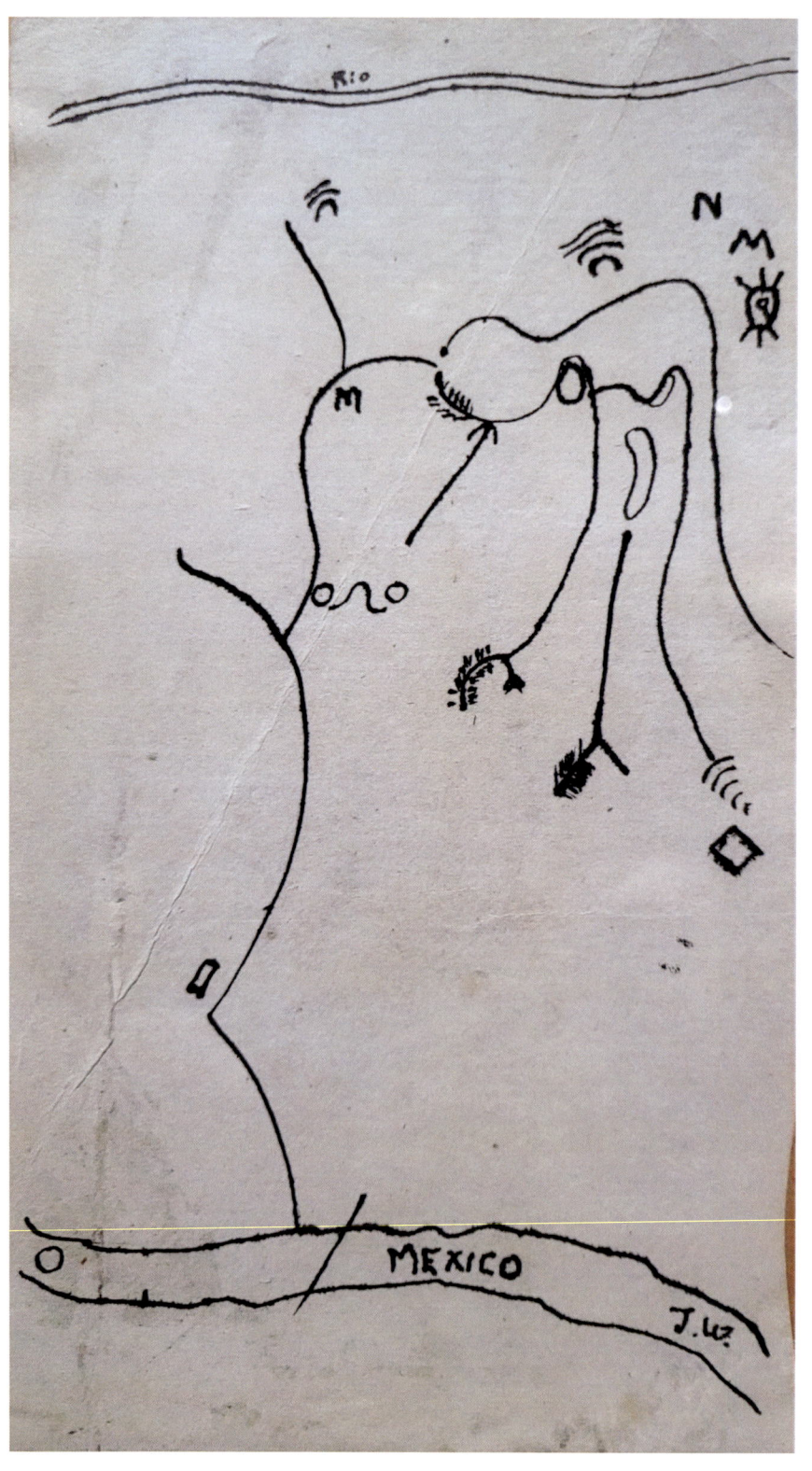

Figure 41- J.W. Map

The origins of this map remain unclear. The initials most likely meant to appear as if they belonged to Jacob Waltz, though this appears to be a copy of an older original. In any case, it is one of the cruder examples. Once again, the mapmakers employed familiar tricks to hide the true location, misidentifying the ravine as "Rio" and incorrectly placing the mine just north of the Mexican border.

Yet, the route marked on this map closely aligns with those depicted in the others. Some of these maps mislabel Randolph Canyon as either Rio Salado or Mexican territory, or they suggest the mine lies near the Rio Salado River when it is really situated much farther south.

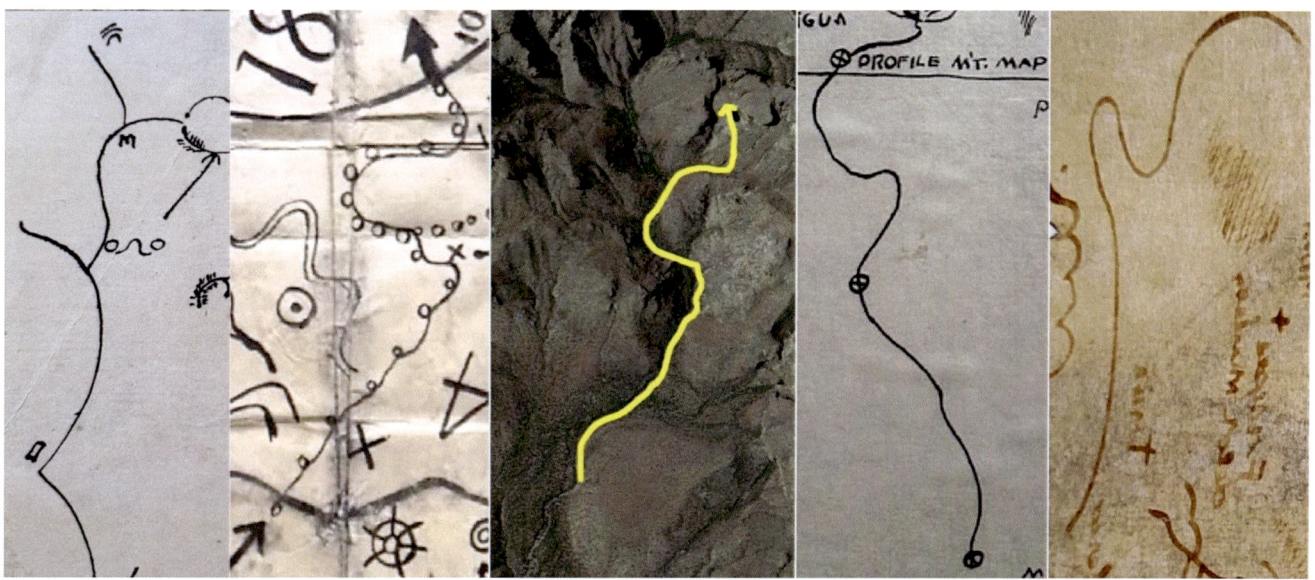

Figure 42- Similarities between each map's path and the Google Earth path (center)

All these maps, with the true path at their center, depict a similar route (Figure 42). The trail on the far right of the image was flipped from its original orientation (Figure 37) to adjust its direction. Each one obscures the real names of landmarks or directions in its own way, requiring a unique method to decode them. To interpret them correctly, you'd need guidance from those already familiar with the path, as they never provide a straightforward key. As Indiana Jones famously said, "We do not follow maps to buried treasure, and 'X' never marks the spot." That holds true for most of these maps, though there are still a few remaining to explore, including the one leading to Jacob Waltz's hidden gold ore.

Gonzalez Mexican Mine Map

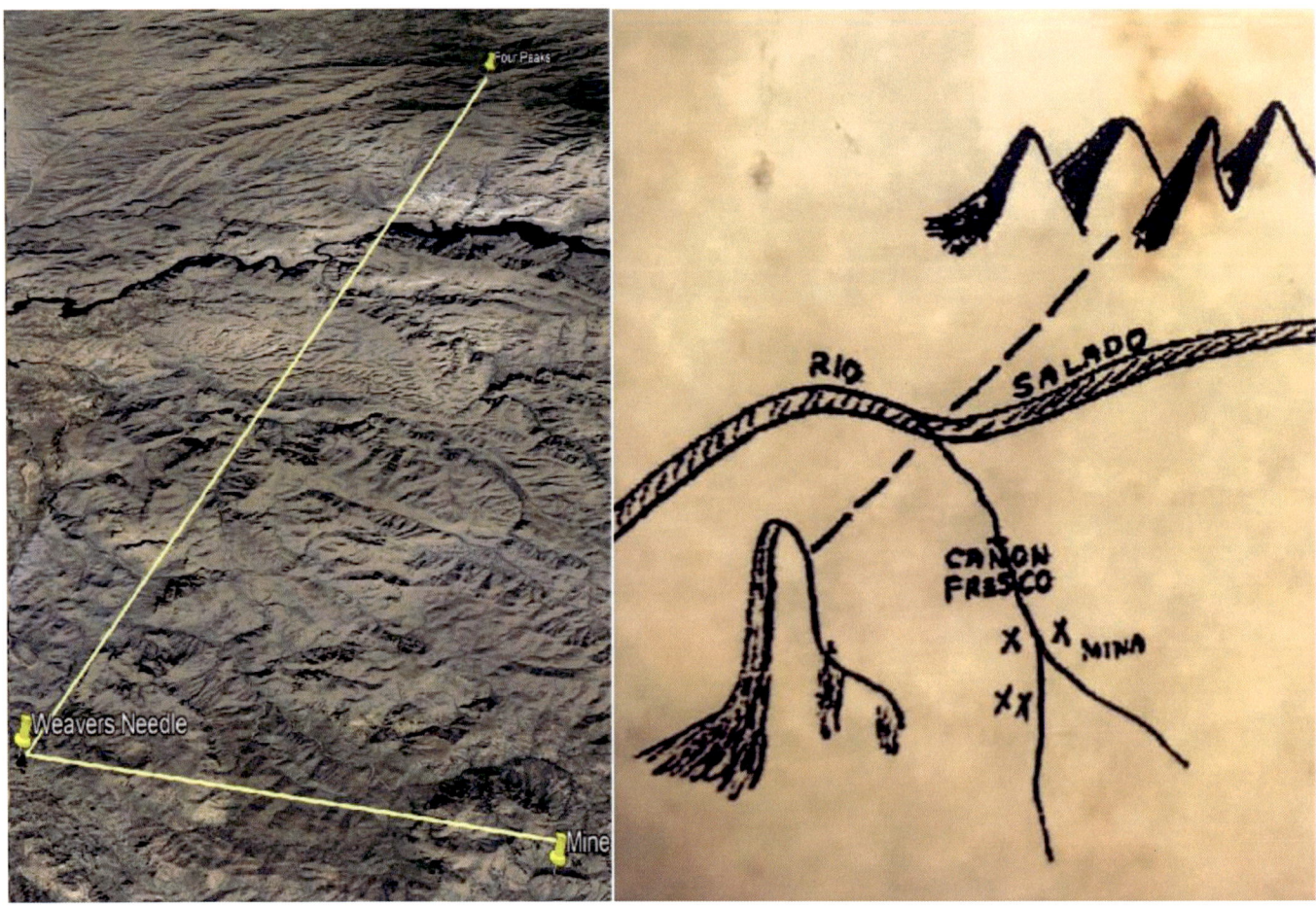

Figure 43- Google Earth image compared to Gonzalez Mexican Mine Map

Another frequently mentioned map is the Gonzalez Mexican Mine Map. While it points toward the general area, it isn't meant to pinpoint the mine's exact location. The proportional distances between Weaver's Needle and Four Peaks match those between Weaver's Needle and my newly discovered Lost Dutchman Mine. Without prior suspicion of that specific area, it's unlikely anyone would have found the mine. Most would assume the heart-shaped mesa marked the spot, just as Abe Reid once did.

The Jacob Waltz Doodle Map

Figure 44- Jacob Waltz gave this map to Julia Thomas to find his cache of gold

At this point, we come to the question of the three caches of gold ore that Jacob Waltz and his partner, Jacob Weiser, hid near the mine. There are doubts about whether Jacob Weiser ever existed, or whether Jacob Waltz had a partner at all. Accounts of these caches were recorded by those who knew Waltz: Jim Bark, who owned the Quarter Circle U Ranch where the Board House was located, and Ely Sims, a newsman and friend of Bark's; and Brownie Holmes, the son of Dick Holmes, who was reportedly at Waltz's bedside when he died. There was also Julia Thomas and her informally adopted son, Rhinehart Petrasch, both of whom cared for Waltz in his final weeks. Their account of Waltz's story was shared with Bark and Ely.

According to Julia Thomas, as Waltz's health deteriorated in early 1891, he shared details of the mine with her and Rhinehart hoping they might help him make one last trip. Unfortunately, he died in October before they could help him return to the mine. Before his death, Jacob Waltz drew a simple map intended to guide them to his camp and the cache (Figure 44). There's no definitive proof that Waltz drew it, but as you'll see, he almost certainly did. Rhinehart and Julia never succeeded in finding the cache, and the map has been misinterpreted by many Dutch hunters who searched endlessly in the Superstition Mountains.

The map shows a pointed mountain adjacent to Waltz's camp. The common interpretation has been that the pointed mountain on the right is Weaver's Needle. It even resembles Weaver's Needle, as shown in Figure 45.

Figure 45- Storm Highlights: Arizona's Weavers Needle; taken by Jeff Swensen (Flickr), used with permission

However, Waltz's map does not show Weaver's Needle; it depicts a different landmark along with other clues meant to guide Rhinehart Petrasch to the camp and the cache. Notably, the mountain on the map has an 'oven mitt' shape, and it includes what appears to be a trail loop. Waltz had mentioned that his camp was situated on the trail above a ravine that leads to the mine. He also stated that he buried his cache near his camp, just above the wash leading to the mine. Below is a Google Earth map of Randolph Canyon, showing an expanded view of the area. The location of the cache lies near the center of this map. At the bottom, left corner is the glove-shaped mountain near Coffee Flat Canyon, and at the top, we see the heart-shaped feature we've discussed earlier.

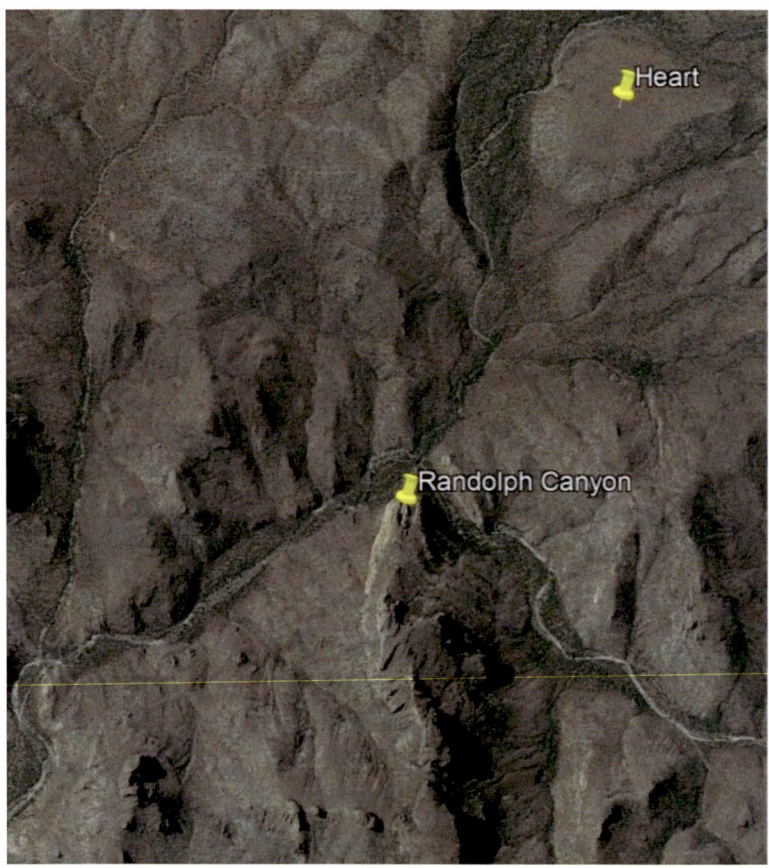

Figure 46- Google Earth image showing Randolph Canyon, also area that is depicted on the Doodle Map

Figure 47- Image of oven mitt peak found on Jacob Waltz Doodle Map just east of Coffee Flat Canyon

The circled mountain and trail loop appear on the Doodle Map. This area lies on the path to the heart and the mine.

Figure 48- Google Earth image of area depicted in Jacob Waltz Doodle Map, peak and Coffee Flat Canyon circled

The Google Earth map shows landmarks such as mountains, riverbeds, and trails that Jacob Waltz sketched on his map.

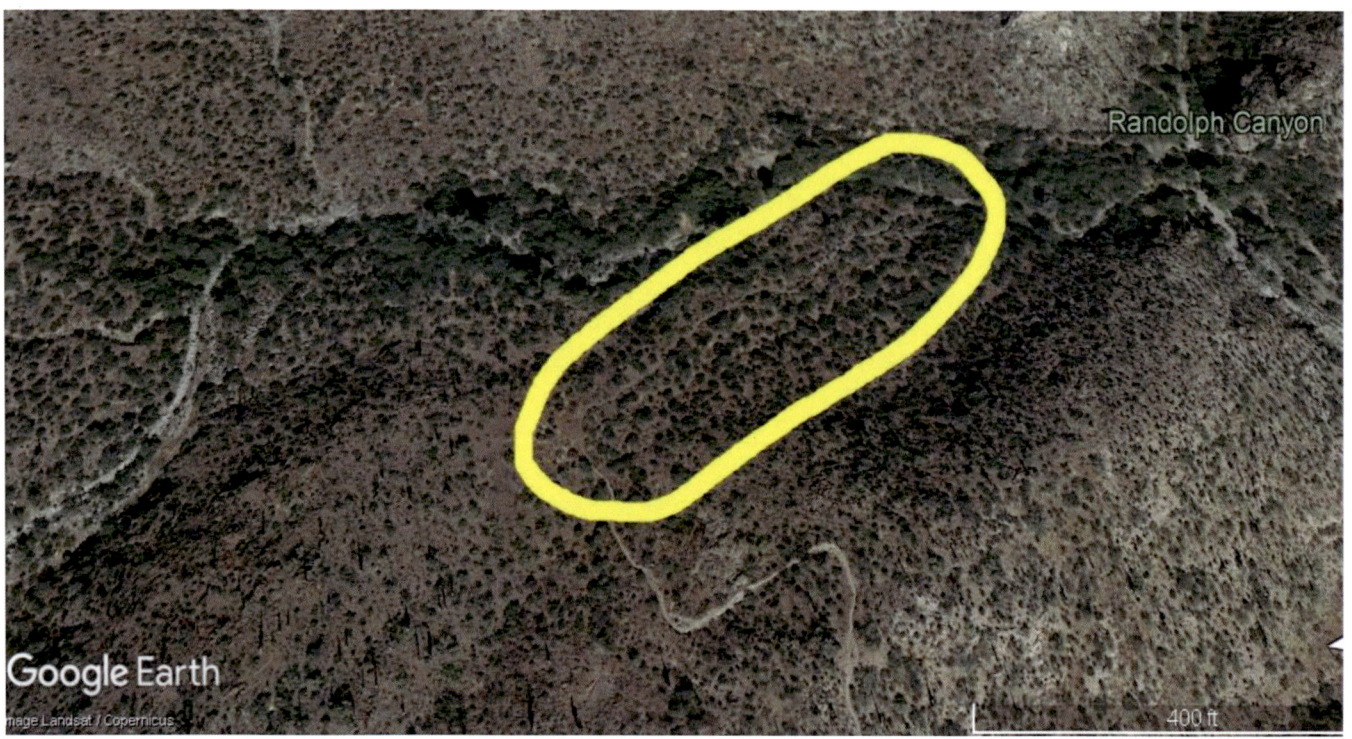

Figure 49- Google Earth image showing path at which Jacob Waltz camped

Waltz camped somewhere in the path before it turned west towards what is now known as the Quarter Circle U Ranch (Figure 49).

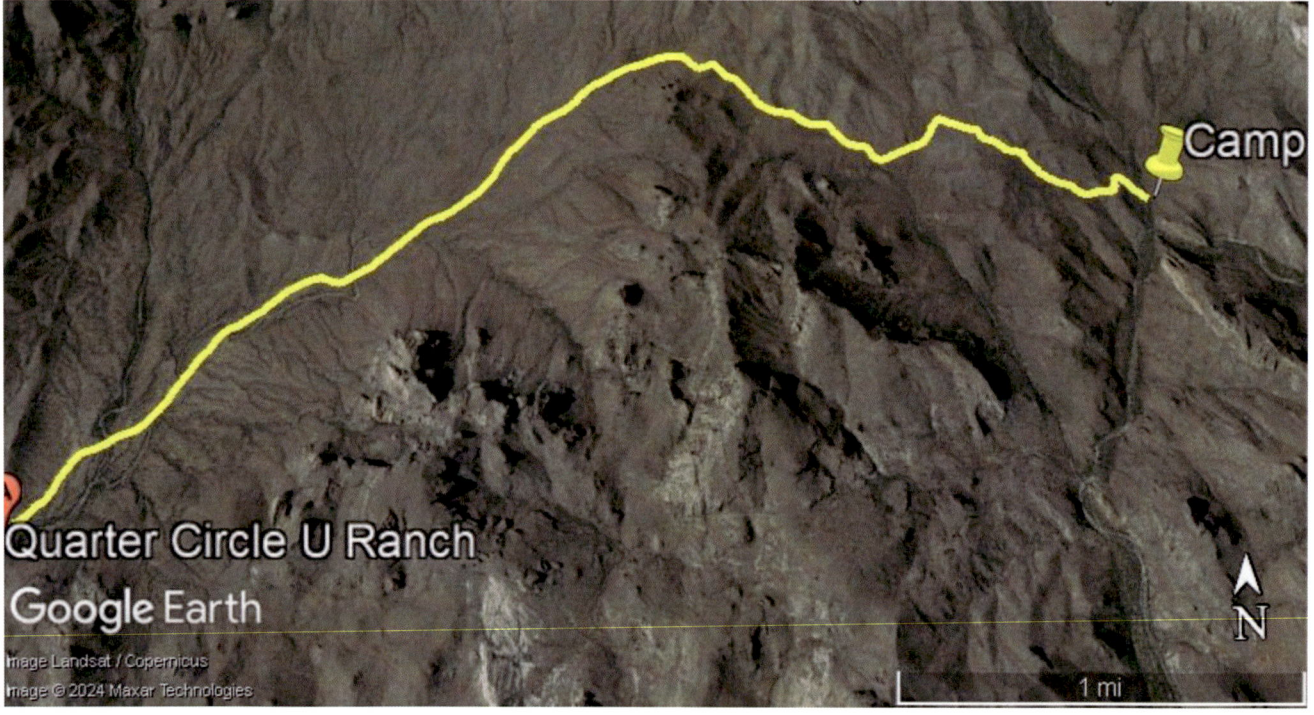

Figure 50- Google Earth image showing probable path Jacob Waltz took from Quarter Circle U Ranch

This is the path Jacob Waltz took from the Board House to his camp, though he may have used other routes to mislead anyone trying to follow him (Figure 50).

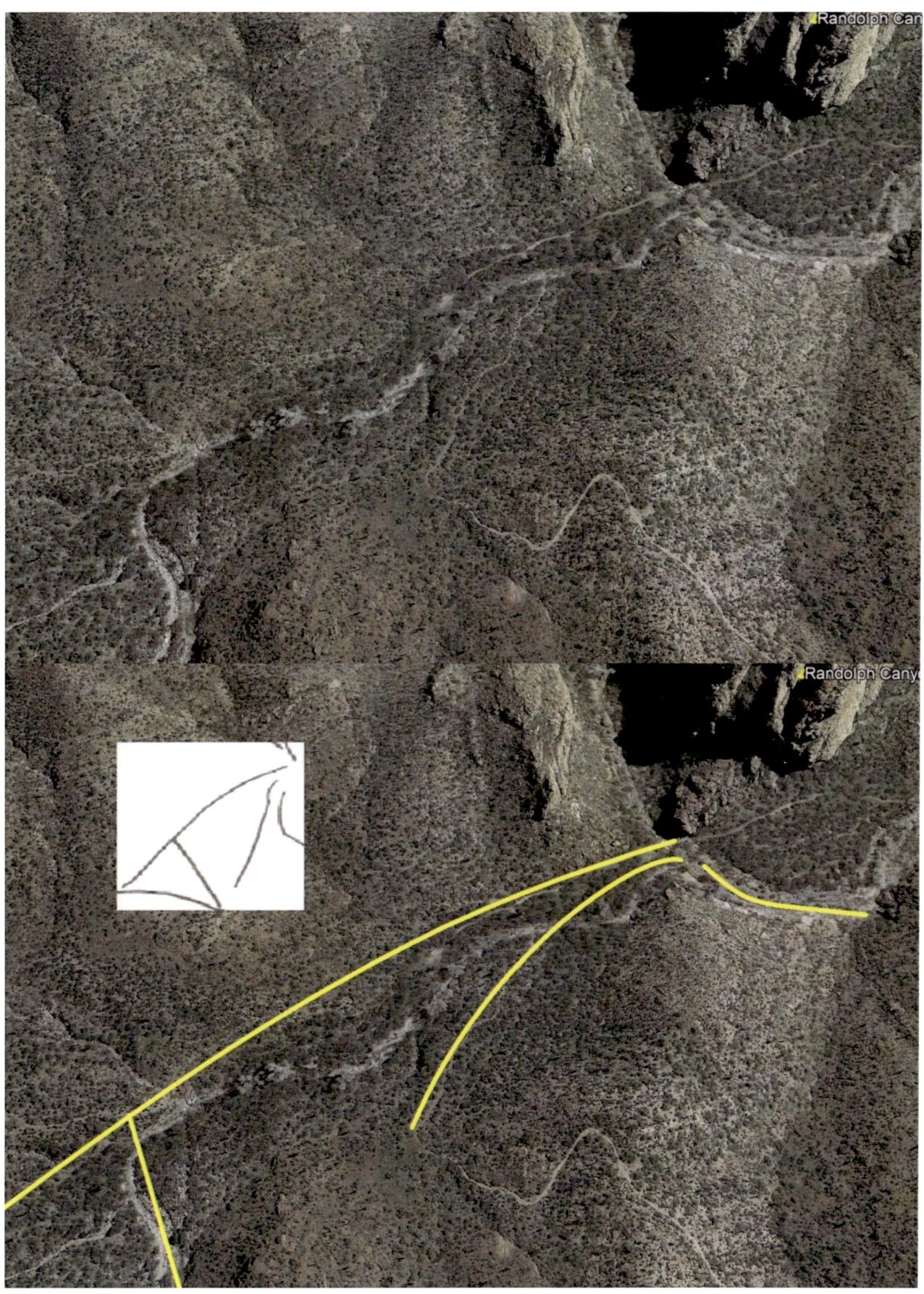

Figure 51- Google Earth image showing map area with ravines matching drawing.

Figure 52- Highlighted area showing path Jacob Waltz camped and buried his cache

Below is the location of Jacob Waltz's camp and the area where he reportedly buried his cache of gold ore. I searched this area, approximately two acres (87,000 sq ft), but found no gold. However, I did discover a large depression that appeared to be the site of a previous excavation. Without a metal detector, it's impossible to determine what lies buried there. Nonetheless, I am now certain that someone had gotten the cache before me.

Figure 53- Google Earth image showing the area where Jacob Waltz camped and buried his cache

"If you can find the camp, you can find the mine."

The quote above offers a major clue left by Jacob Waltz. Well, I reversed that course and found the mine first, which led me to his famous buried cache. Unfortunately, as noted, it is likely that the cache had already been discovered.

Another key character in this saga is Travis Tumlinson, whom I believe, along with a couple others, found the cache. His discovery adds another colorful chapter to the story. Tumlinson was rumored to have found a million dollars' worth of cobbled gold in the Millsite Hewitt Canyon area, though I suspect he found it along the path leading out of Randolph Canyon. We'll explore that part of the legend in the next chapter. We will also delve into the tales of Bob Garman, the Depression-era Dutch hunter, and Adolph Ruth, the ill-fated treasure seeker who perished mysteriously in the mountains. The only reason we know about the Doodle Map is because of how closely Bob Garman was connected to the Petrasch family. He was likely one of the few people who even knew it existed. Once he, Reid, and Tumlinson deciphered it, there was no longer any reason to keep it secret, so they let it out.

As for Abe Reid, there's only one reason for him to dig where he did: he had the Peralta Heart Map. He dug where the arrow on the Peralta Heart Map pointed. We'll explore how he came to possess the map and how he is connected to Adolph Ruth. But before that, let's take a small detour and touch on the story of the two soldiers.

The Two Soldiers Story

In addition to the Lost Dutchman Mine legends, there's also the tale of the two soldiers. As Thomas Glover recounts the story (based on notes taken by Bark and Ely), the soldiers had been discharged from the army at Fort McDowell. They decided to seek work at the Silver King Mine, 40 miles southeast, where wages were higher. They traveled mostly through ravines, climbing mountains only to orient themselves. Along the way, they stumbled upon a mine and its tailings. There, they found handfuls of gold nuggets and stuffed their pockets with them.

When the superintendent of the Silver King Mine learned of their find, he persuaded them to return to the mine to collect more, offering to partner with them. Equipped with two burros and gear, they were to retrace their steps to the gold mine. There's a chance they found one of the mines adjacent to the Lost Dutchman Mine (Figure 54).

Figure 54- Google Earth image showing the mine and a line drawn from Fort McDowell to Silver King Mine

It is widely believed that these two men reached Randolph Canyon, just below the heart-shaped mesa, and continued traveling east. The consensus is that they found the mine earlier in their journey and had already collected gold. In my opinion, they likely headed southeast along Whiskey Spring Trail to the mountain north of the Dutchman Mine, where they discovered a mine and its tailings. Afterward, they probably traveled south to Randolph Canyon and then east toward the Silver King Mine. After partnering with the superintendent and setting off to relocate the mine, they were never heard from again. One of the men was reportedly found dead shortly afterward, suggesting they failed to return to the mine.

The Holmes Map

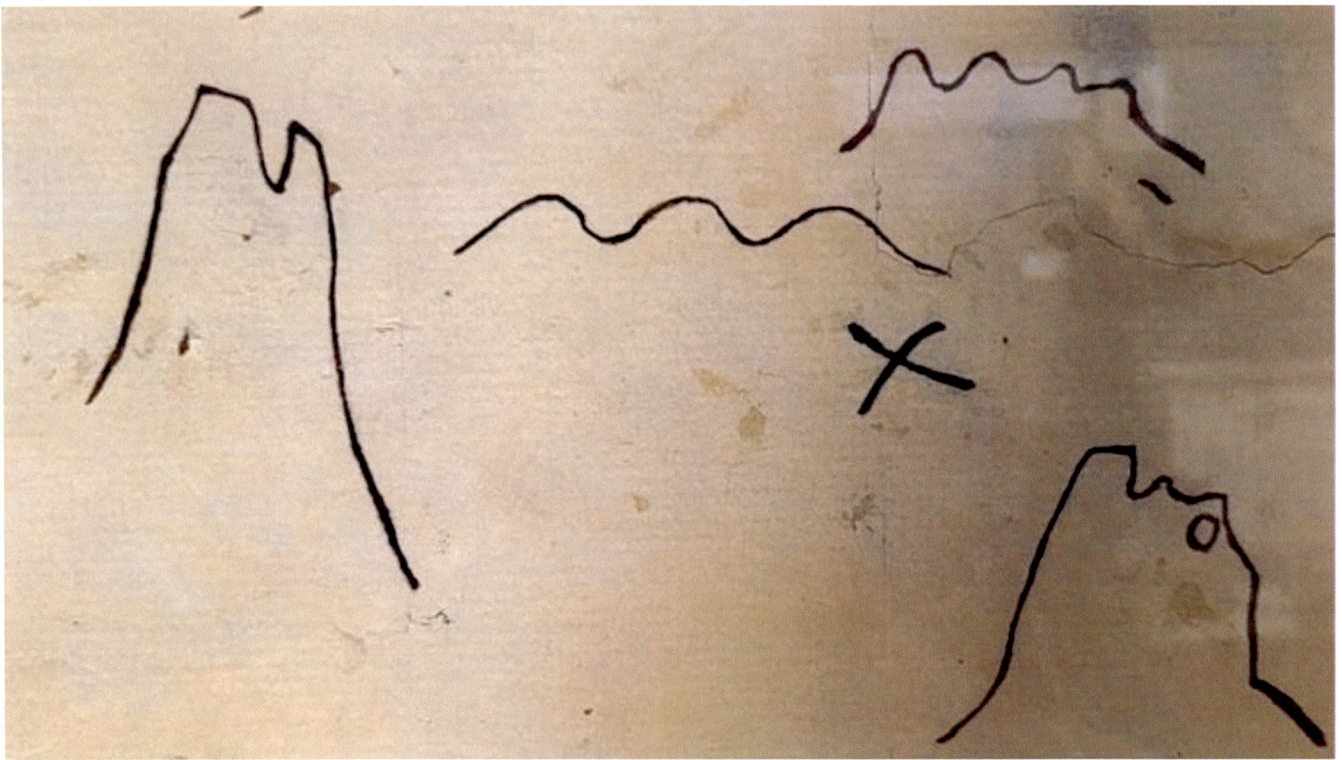

Figure 55- The Holmes Map

This map is believed to have been created by Dick Holmes and Gideon Roberts. According to Brownie Holmes, Dick's son, Jacob Waltz attempted to give Dick directions to the mine as he lay dying. However, Waltz didn't intend to lead them directly to the mine, only to its general vicinity. When examining the map, many assume that the peak on the left represents Weaver's Needle. But, like every map we've seen so far, this one has its secrets. The map may have been intentionally altered before being shared, obscuring the true location. Perhaps Jacob Waltz even drew it himself before his death.

I suspect that the glove-shaped peak on the left of the map is the same one Waltz sketched on his Doodle Map. Although the peaks resemble Weaver's Needle, they are distinct landmarks. By flipping the Holmes Map and using the glove-shaped peak as a landmark, instead of Weaver's Needle, the map more accurately reveals the true location of Jacob's camp and cache (Figure 56).

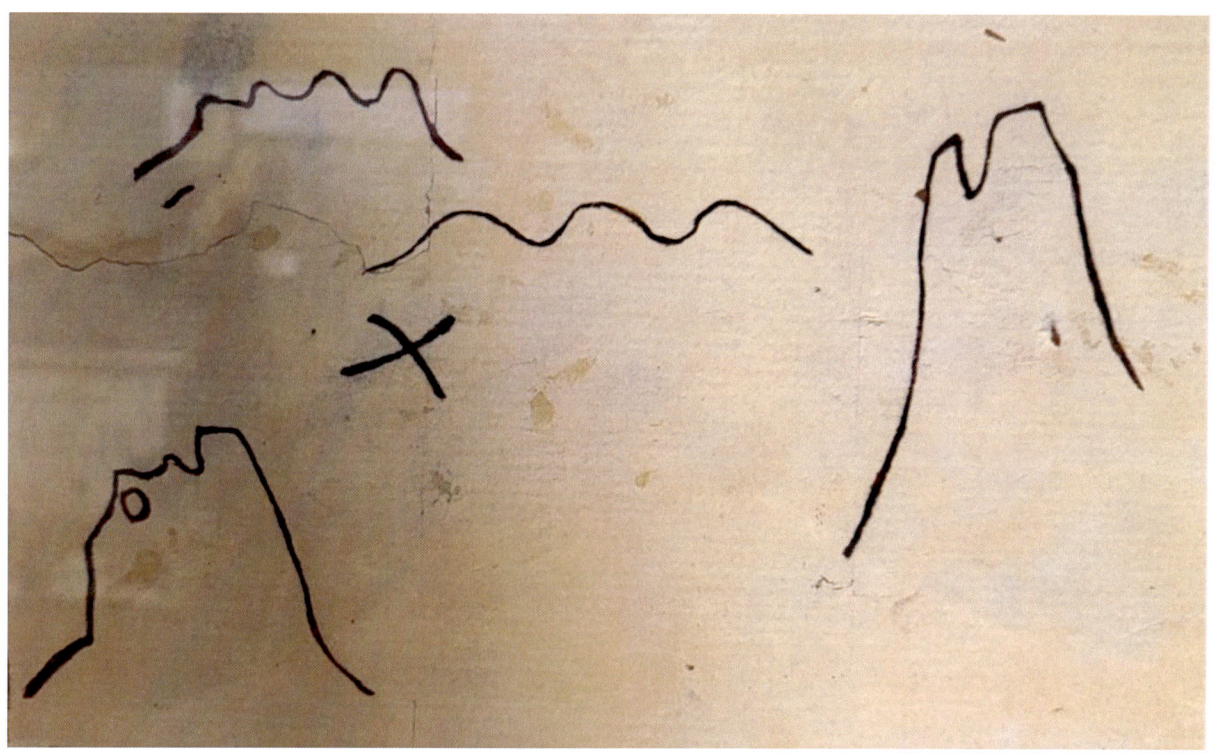

Figure 56- Holmes Map, reversed

Figure 57- Close up of Miners Needle P1000606 by Bill Incognito (Flickr), used with permission

Figure 58- Google Earth image of area depicted in reversed Holmes Map

Figure 58 shows the Google Earth image of the area using the reversed Dick Holmes Map (Figure 56). The two match perfectly. The three hills from the map are visible in Figure 59. As Jacob Waltz said: "If you pass three red hills, you've gone too far." The mine sits atop those hills. But remember, the map wasn't meant to lead directly to the mine, only to bring seekers near Jacob's buried cache.

Figure 59- Google Earth image showing the mine atop the three hills, a likely reference to the "three red hills" clue

Adolph Ruth and Abe Reid

At this point, we return to the story of Adolph Ruth, the Depression-era treasure hunter whose remains were discovered in 1932. His story is closely tied to that of Abe Reid, a contemporary described by Clay Worst and Richard Glover as "one of the last of the true old-timers of the mountains."

Many theories surround Ruth's death, but a few facts are clear. In June 1931, Adolph Ruth left the Quarter Circle U Ranch carrying old Spanish maps that his son had acquired in Mexico. Ruth was seventy-eight years old, frail, and walked with a cane due to a lingering injury. Despite his physical condition, he convinced two ranch hands, Jack Keenan and Leroy Purnell, to help guide him into the Superstition Mountains. According to the cowboys, Ruth set up camp at Willow Springs in Boulder Canyon. It was the last place anyone reported seeing him alive.

On June 20, 1931, William "Tex" Barkley, owner of the Quarter Circle U Ranch, visited Ruth's campsite to check on him. Barkley noted that Ruth had been gone for at least twenty-four hours and promptly reported the disappearance to the authorities.

This is where Abe Reid enters the story. Although many who knew Reid spoke highly of him and dismissed any suggestion of wrongdoing, the circumstances surrounding Adolph Ruth's disappearance raise serious questions about Reid's involvement. I cannot say with absolute certainty that Reid killed Ruth, but the evidence strongly suggests he was directly involved in his death. At a minimum, Reid appears to have encountered Ruth's body and taken possession of the Peralta Heart Map. Reid was reportedly seen carrying a body on horseback heading west shortly before Ruth was reported missing and later claimed to have transported the body from its discovery site back to the authorities.

There is limited information about Abe Reid available online. According to Reid himself, he discovered the Cursum Perficio Map (Figure 60) tucked inside an old Jesuit prayer book at a library in Phoenix. The book, the third volume of a three-part series titled *Concionum Sanctis*, was written by Fr. Juan de Osorio, a Spanish Jesuit (1542–1594), and contains texts in both Latin and Spanish.

It is likely that Reid invented this story to justify his possession of the maps. With his knowledge of local legends and Jesuit lore, he may have borrowed elements from old religious texts to give his claims an air of legitimacy. It's entirely possible that he did visit a library and found some obscure Jesuit volumes but then used that discovery to support a fabricated narrative. I am not alone in doubting Reid's version of events. Tom Kollenborn, a well-respected authority on the Superstition Mountains, also expressed skepticism. After studying the book, Kollenborn remained unconvinced, noting that Reid's story did not align with known historical facts about the region.

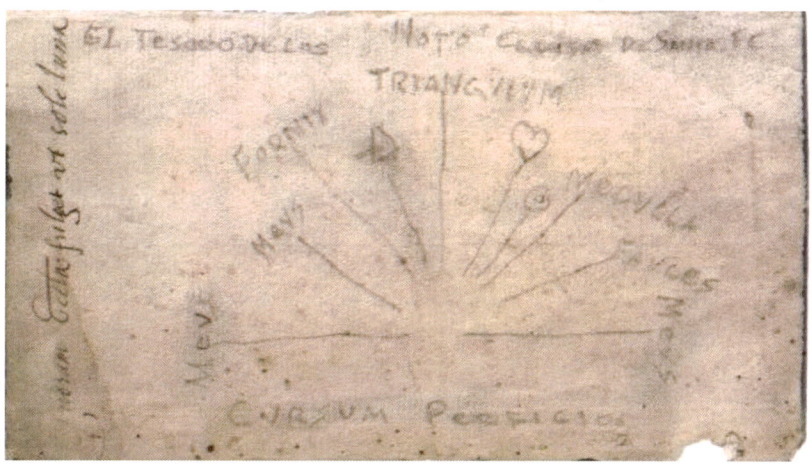

Figure 60- Cursum Perficio Map purportedly found by Abe Reid in a library

Unfortunately for Abe, he couldn't correctly decipher the maps and began digging where the arrow pointed on the Peralta Heart Map (Figure 61a). The heart-shaped mesa shows no unique features suggesting gold or silver presence. Many found it odd that he chose this spot to dig.

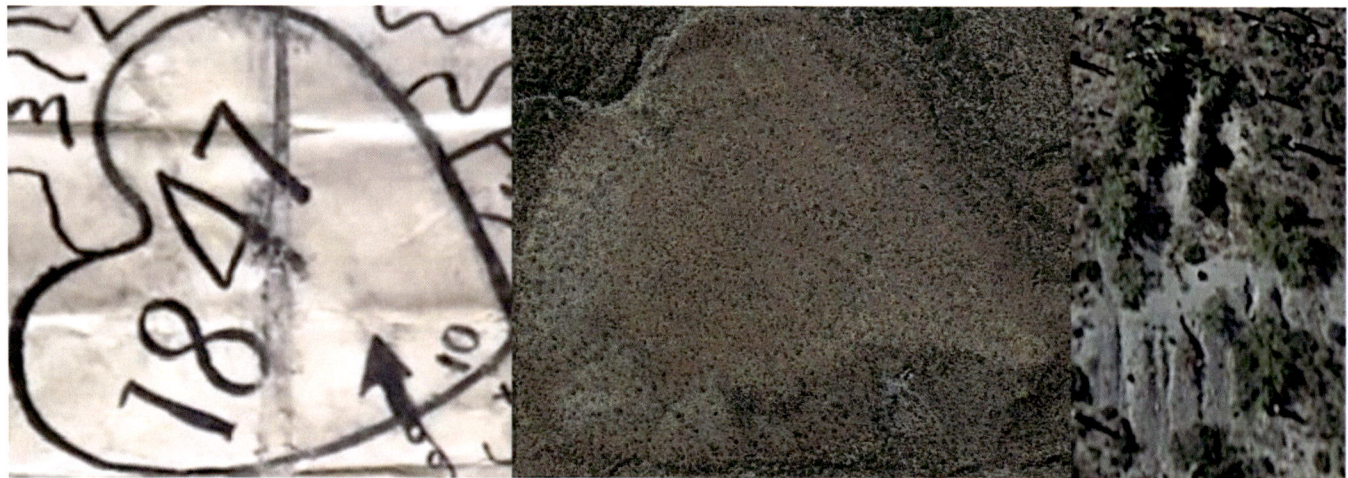

Figure 61a- Heart on the Peralta Heart Map and Google Earth image of the heart formation, with close-up of digging

I believe Reid would only have dug in that location if he had the map in his possession

I also find it difficult to believe Reid acted entirely on his own. Ruth could not have hiked seven miles over rugged terrain in June with only a single canteen of water, nor is there evidence he ever found or even came close to the mine by himself. It is far more likely that Ruth chose the Quarter Circle U Ranch because it provided relatively easy access to Randolph Canyon, where he intended to establish his camp. From there, Keenan and Purnell appear to have guided him east and helped set up a camp near Randolph Canyon. That, however, seems to have been the end of Ruth's journey.

One explanation is that Reid later stumbled upon Ruth's body, took possession of the maps, gathered the remains, and instructed the two cowboys to relocate the camp. While this scenario is possible, it leaves too many questions unanswered. Most notably, it fails to satisfactorily explain the gunshot-like wound observed in Ruth's skull (Figure 61b). Although the official investigation suggested the holes may have resulted from a fall, that conclusion has long been disputed. An unsigned report attributed to Dr. Alex Herlicka concluded that Ruth died from a gunshot wound to the head; a finding that Arizona authorities never formally accepted. Many have argued the case was never properly investigated, particularly in the context of 1930s Phoenix, where political influence, land ownership, and law enforcement were often closely connected.

There was also an eyewitness that implicates Abe Reid. Ted Cox claimed to have seen Abe Reid traveling west with a body packed on a horse. Ron Feldman, who now possesses Cox's notes, along with his sons, has published extensively based on that testimony. Taken together, these details strongly suggest Reid's involvement went beyond a chance discovery. Whether he caused Ruth's death or encountered the body afterward, Reid appears to have taken control of the situation, the maps, and the narrative itself. The reader must decide which explanation best fits the evidence.

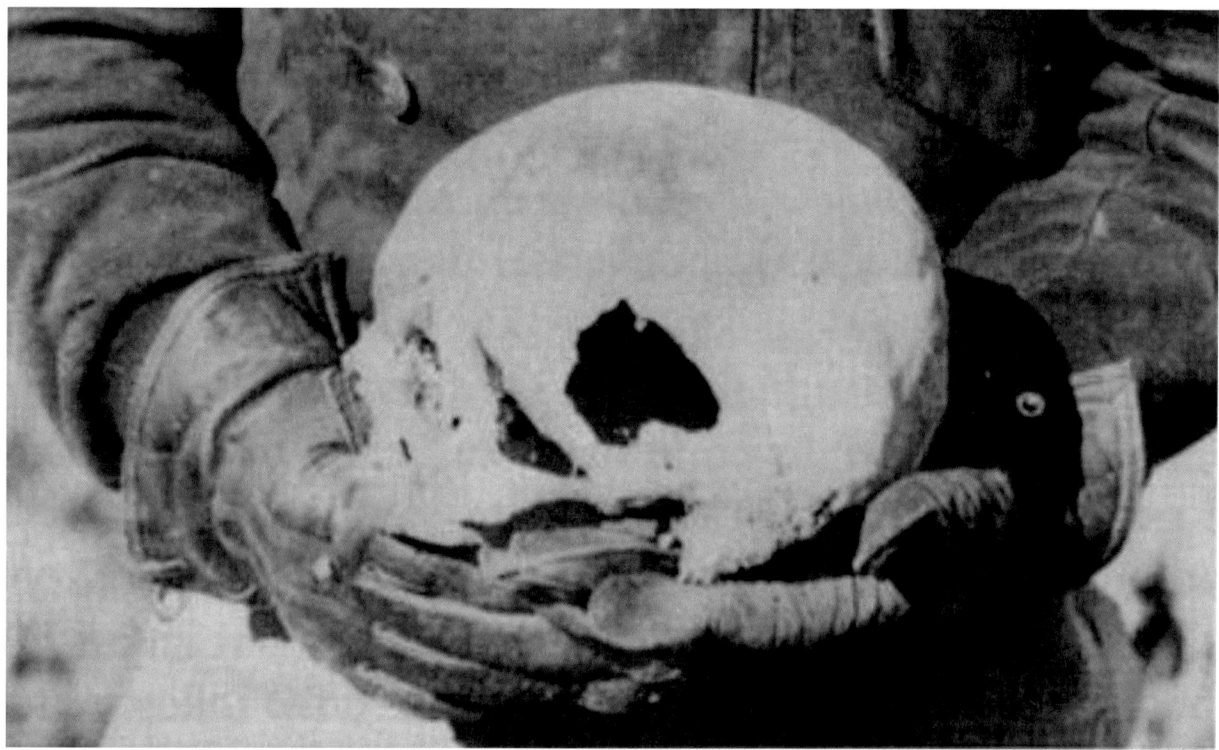

Figure 61b- Closeup of Adolph Ruth's skull held by Brownie Holmes

This also helps explain why Abe Reid continued digging around Randolph Canyon, where he had camped for more than twenty years. He told others he was mining for low-grade silver and even published a map to his mine, which he called Silver Belle. Everyone knew there was no silver in that area, but they didn't have the heart to tell "Good ol' Abe." George W. Kollenborn, Tom's father and a close friend of Reid, once told Tom he never understood why Abe chose that particular spot, since no silver deposits were known to exist there. Locals likely saw him working on that washed-out hill and shook their heads, saying, "Why's he digging that ditch like some failed '49er? Trying to strike it rich, but he's just a miner."

I am fairly certain that most of the Peralta maps discussed here once belonged to Adolph Ruth. The map that appears to have captured Abe Reid's interest was the Peralta Heart Map. Originally created and used by the Peralta family as a guide, it was later passed to Pedro Gonzalez, who was said to be related to the Peraltas. Gonzalez traded the Heart Map, along with several others, to Erwin C. Ruth in exchange for legal assistance. Erwin then gave the maps to his father, Adolph Ruth, who carried them into the Superstitions during his ill-fated 1931 expedition.

Following Ruth's suspicious death, Abe Reid came into possession of the maps and spent years digging at a mine that ultimately proved empty. After many unsuccessful attempts to find gold, Reid shared the maps with Travis Tumlinson. Once Tumlinson became convinced he had located the cache, the Peralta Heart Map was no longer considered essential and was passed to George W. Kollenborn, then to Tom Kollenborn, and eventually to Frank Augustine.

Most of the known Peralta maps did not surface publicly until the mid to late 1950s, likely because by that time those involved believed the cache, and possibly the mine itself, had already been found and the maps were no longer needed.

Some of this is speculative, but I believe this sequence fits the available evidence.

Travis and Robert Tumlinson

By the 1950s, Abe Reid had already spent nearly twenty years digging at his so-called silver mine with little to show for it. Growing increasingly desperate, as I believe, Abe reached out to the Tumlinson family for help deciphering the map. The Tumlinsons were well known in treasure-hunting circles, particularly for their ornate stone carvings and hand-drawn maps. Travis likely met with Reid to discuss the map, and together they realized they needed someone with deeper knowledge of the area. To assist, Bob Garman was brought on board. Garman had extensive knowledge of the Dutchman legend and the surrounding terrain and spent several years searching the nearby canyons. He was also a close friend of Herman Petrasch, the brother of Rhinehart Petrasch, who famously searched for the mine with Julia Thomas after Jacob Waltz's death.

This theory is supported by a firsthand account from Tom Kollenborn, who said he was with Bob Garman when they met Robert Tumlinson and two others in Randolph Canyon in the early 1950s. This was the same location where Abe Reid had established his long-time camp, a spot still known as Reid's Water (Figure 62). Abe lived there year-round until he died in 1958. The two unnamed individuals were likely Travis and his maternal uncle, Phil Leasman

Figure 62- Google Earth image of Randolph Canyon.

Later, Garman and Tumlinson each claimed to have found a stone tablet etched with a version of the Heart Map. Their stories changed over time, with each initially taking credit before eventually attributing the find to Travis. Travis later claimed to have discovered additional tablets, some of which he sold privately while others were donated to museums. However, many Dutch hunters consider the Tumlinsons' story to be a fabrication. People like Frank Augustine recall being shown early photographs and blueprints of what appeared to be preliminary versions of the maps.

I believe Tumlinson, Lessman, and Garman successfully decoded Jacob Waltz's Doodle Map and realized it pointed to Randolph Canyon. They may have extracted the remaining gold, either shortly before or just after Abe Reid died. Once they had the treasure, the maps no longer mattered, and they probably gave them away. The Peralta Heart Map, for example, was later given to George Kollenborn. Since Reid had never found gold, they likely assumed Waltz had already exhausted the deposit. I'm sure they didn't tell Reid about their find, though.

It is important to understand this point. The Stone Maps are fake, well, sort of. They are not ancient maps from antiquity, but modern creations. They are meant to guide the treasure hunter to where Travis **thought** the mine was, the heart-shaped mesa. Many Dutch hunters can get stuck on this and will stop reading if they think I am suggesting the maps are real. Since Travis was successful in figuring out the Dutchman's Doodle Map and believed all the gold was accounted for, he didn't need to protect the secret. This probably inspired Travis to start creating and selling stone maps. These maps became both a source of income and a cover story for his sudden wealth from discovering the cache.

Figure 63- The Stone Map of the Heart. It is now on view at the Superstition Mountain Museum.

These ornate stone maps mimic the kinds of maps the Tumlinson family was known for. Travis's grandfather, Pegleg Tumlinson, was a well-known treasure hunter and map collector. A good example of their craft is the Stone

Horse Map. Travis copied the horse shape directly from a 1904 topographic map of the Florence Quadrangle. This area lies along the southern edge of the Superstitions, about forty miles east of Phoenix. The resemblance between the map's stylized horsehead and Tumlinson's carving is hard to miss. They adapted the outlined horsehead from this map, using it as the model for their Stone Map carving.

Figure 64- Stone Horse Map created by Travis Tumlinson

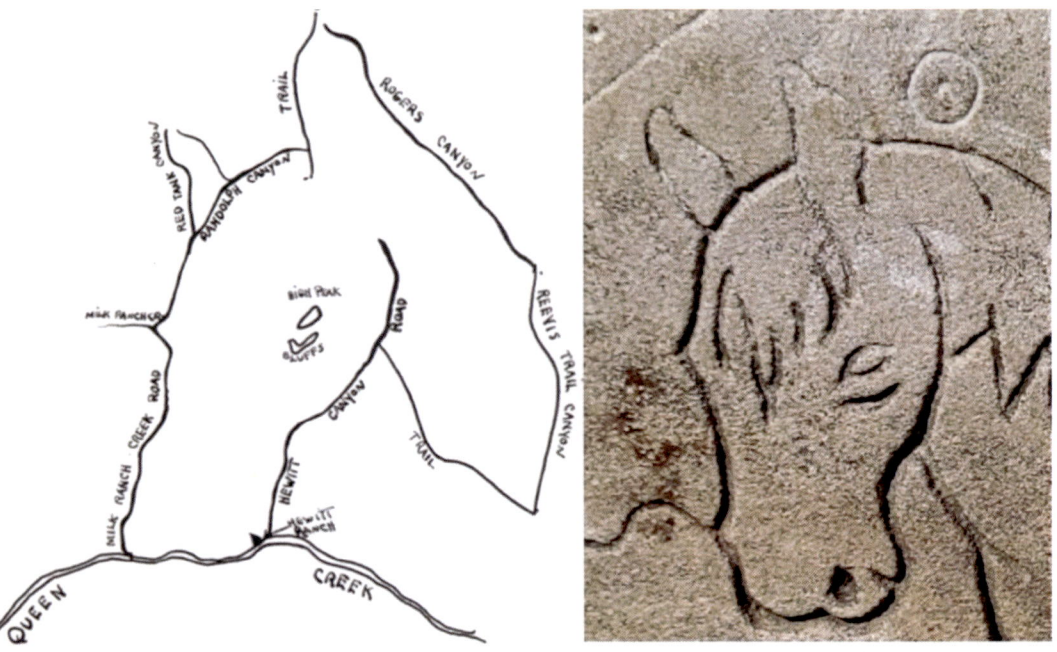

Figure 65- Frontier Times drawing of the Florence Quadrangle Map of 1904, from which the figure of the horse head was taken.

On the Stone Map, a double circle near the horse's ear is said to represent the mine (Figure 65). The original 1904 map was more artistic than scientific, with the horse shape added by a creative cartographer. Tumlinson mimicked that shape and made adjustments to match any trail features he had observed. He also included a well-known local landmark, Elephant Butte.

Figure 66- Frontier Times artist's rendition showing how to move the elephant Trunk under ear which lines up with mine to the north.

In one interpretation, moving the elephant's trunk under its leg causes the eye of the elephant to line up with the spot Tumlinson believed was the mine, marked by the double circle (Figure 66). This theory comes from an article in the April–May 1973 issue of *Frontier Times*. That article explains how Tumlinson got the idea and provides diagrams of the adjustments, so full credit goes to them.

Many Dutch hunters today are aware of the connection to Elephant Butte. Most people scoff at the idea because it is widely accepted that the Stone Maps are fake. But both sides have a point. The maps are fake, but they do point to a real place: the heart formation. Unfortunately, those who believe the maps are genuine have overlooked how far north Tumlinson believed the heart, and therefore the mine, was located.

The image below overlays the Florence Quadrangle's horse path with modern Google Earth imagery. It outlines the route the horse-head maps were trying to show. The heart formation is clearly visible just north of Elephant Butte.

Figure 67- Outline of horse head superimposed over Google Earth image of the terrain based on Quadrangle Map of 1904

Tumlinson also forged other stone maps, including one often referred to as the Priest Map (Figure 68). An article in *Frontier Times* claims that Tumlinson embedded geographic coordinates and even encoded the name "Tonto National Forest" into the carvings. While I haven't fully deciphered the Priest Map to confirm that detail, I consider it largely irrelevant. From what I can tell, Tumlinson copied the central figure from one of his daughter's comic books. Below is a snapshot from Larry Hedrick's video discussing the stone maps and the comic book that Travis used as inspiration. As you can see, it featured a witch, not a priest. These maps were created after the Peralta Stone Maps, likely as souvenir items that Tumlinson could sell to enthusiastic treasure hunters.

Figure 68- Comparison of the Stone Map 'priest' figure (left) with a comic book witch (right) courtesy of Larry Hedrick.

According to legend, Travis Tumlinson discovered cobbled gold valued at one million dollars in the Millsite Hewitt area. This treasure was the actual cache hidden by the Lost Dutchman. Tumlinson, along with his uncle Phil and Bob Garman, likely decoded Jacob Waltz's Doodle Map and found the gold. They split the discovery among themselves, leaving Abe Reid out entirely.

The lingering question is why Tumlinson would create and distribute a map that pointed to what he thought was the mine. His true motivation remains unclear. One theory suggests that he wanted to distance himself from Adolph Ruth's mysterious death and to prevent the government from seizing the gold. I suspect that the trio, Tumlinson, Leasman, and Garman, discovered the Dutchman's stash somewhere along the trail above Randolph Canyon, while Abe Reid continued to dig hopelessly in the wrong spot. They kept their find a secret until after Reid's death. Once Reid was gone and the treasure was secure, Tumlinson no longer had any reason to stay quiet.

This is likely why Tumlinson and Garman eventually made their version of the map public. Tumlinson followed up by crafting the Stone Maps, perhaps as a distraction or to explain his sudden wealth. At the time, President Roosevelt's Executive Order 6102 had made private gold ownership illegal. Tumlinson couldn't legally keep the treasure, so instead, he turned to selling maps and guiding treasure seekers to the general area. All of this allowed him to profit from his find while keeping the truth hidden. In the end, neither Tumlinson nor Reid correctly decoded the Peralta Heart Map, which led them to search in the wrong place.

The Runaround

All the clues were falling into place. What I saw on the maps aligned perfectly with the clues that Jacob Waltz left behind, much of which I have already discussed. The mine is located in a north-trending canyon. A rock face shaped like a horse's head marks the entrance. His shaft and the nearby Mexican mine were close to each other, though not visible from one another. He also mentioned ruins at the base of the canyon and a two-room cave located about 200 feet west of the mine.

I sat there, overwhelmed with the realization that I had found the mine based on the clear evidence in front of me. I was elated, but reality quickly set in.

So, what now? What do I do with this discovery? Who do I reach out to?

My mind immediately went to Wayne Tuttle. Remember him? Wayne Tuttle is the local expert on the Lost Dutchman Mine, the guy who made that video I watched on the *History Channel*. I knew he had a Facebook page, so I decided to contact him.

I wrote: "Hey, Wayne, this may sound crazy, but I found something in the desert, and I'd like to get your opinion."

Tuttle never responded, which wasn't surprising. I was growing more desperate by the minute. I needed to share my findings with someone who could validate the evidence. I decided to call him using Facebook Messenger. To my surprise, he answered.

"Wayne," I said, "I know this sounds crazy, but hear me out. I'm 100 percent sure I've found the location of the Lost Dutchman Mine, and I'd like to show you how I came to that conclusion."

He replied, "No, you didn't. I guarantee you didn't find it. People have dedicated their entire lives to searching for it, and they haven't found it."

"I get that," I said. "But this is different. I've solved all the maps, and they all point to the same location."

"That's impossible," he said. "Because those maps you're talking about, they don't all point to the same spot."

"But they do," I insisted.

"No, some say, 'Rio Salado River,' and some are probably referring to New Mexico."

"Some of them do say that," I acknowledged. "But that's not because the river is there. Those maps are designed to mislead and conceal the true location."

"Why would anyone create a map that can't be followed? That doesn't make sense," he said.

"These are Peralta family maps," I explained. "They were made specifically for their family. And they all use similar tricks. For example, the Peralta Heart Map says '1847,' but the Minas de Oro map says '1844.' These are codes meant to obscure the true location, not for anyone else to decipher."

"Send me a picture of the mine, and I'll take a look," he said finally.

I sent him a close-up Google Earth map showing the mine's entrance (Figure 69). He took one brief glance and said, "No, sorry. I don't see any tailings. I don't see anything that indicates it's there. That's not it."

Figure 69- Google Earth Photo, Shadows showing location of the mines.

I couldn't leave it at that. "Wayne, wait a minute," I said. "Is there someone else you can refer me to? Obviously, I need more proof before you'll meet with me. That's fine. But who can I talk to? Someone who can help me, maybe make a recommendation."

He asked me if I'd ever been to Goldfield Ghost Town? I responded "no", and he said I should reach out to the owner, Bob Schoose. He gave me Bob's number and wished me good luck. He also said that if I end up going to that spot in the mountain, to let him know so he'll know where to send the mountain rescue team. I laughed nervously, thanked him, and said goodbye. Wayne seemed genuinely concerned about my safety and reiterated that I mustn't go out there unprepared. I picked up the phone and dialed Bob's number.

Bob Schoose answered the phone right away and I let him know the whole story. He invited me to show him what I found. The next day, I went to Goldfield.

Bob Schoose has served as the unofficial mayor of Goldfield Ghost Town near Arizona's Superstition Mountains for nearly three decades. A natural storyteller, he's built his livelihood around weaving the legend of the Lost Dutchman Mine to captivate visitors. When I met him, he seemed like a living extension of Goldfield's rugged history. His steel-gray hair and wind-worn beard gave him the air of a man who'd spent a lifetime swapping tales around desert campfires, with a scruffy voice to match.

Now picture the scene: Schoose sees me approaching, my arms full of maps and papers. I start with the Profile Map. I had done some research on him and knew that he believed he had already found the mine. Sure enough, as soon as he saw me pull out the Profile Map, he stopped me right there.

"You're one of those numbers guys," he said, referring to the clear notation on the map that read "15,000 E. to W. to N. to S."

"Yeah," I said. "I'm a numbers guy," not entirely sure what that meant. I like numbers. It's got to be a good thing, right?

He said, "Yeah, I can see that. But I've already found this mine. This is in New Mexico."

"No, it's not," I replied.

"Yes, it is. And this is a river," he said, pointing to the curved line in the lower part of the map.

"No, it's not," I said again.

"Yes, it's a river," he insisted.

It became clear to me that this approach wasn't going to work. I needed a different way to present my evidence to Bob Schoose. I gave it one last try.

"Okay, let's assume the Peralta family did own a silver mine in New Mexico called the South Sima, and that they were skilled at concealing the truth in their maps. Think about it. Why would they create a map that was clearly labeled and easy to follow? Look, this even marks the cave across from the mine, which aligns with the Dutchman's clue about a two-room cave near the mine. This must be a map leading to the same Lost Dutchman's mine."

But it was no use. "You're not understanding me," he said.

That was the end of that.

I returned to Wayne Tuttle, pushing him for another contact. I wanted someone who hadn't already convinced themselves they'd discovered the mine. The only suggestion he offered was Jack San Felice, another Dutch hunter who had recently published a book about the legend.

I contacted Jack, generously complimenting his work and explaining how his videos had influenced my research. Eventually, I got straight to the point. I told him I believed I'd pinpointed the mine's location and asked if we could discuss it. I even proposed an arrangement: I would share my research with him, and if he could disprove my findings, I would happily withdraw and purchase a copy of his book.

His response was brief, "The Lost Dutchman Mine lies buried under 75 to 88 feet of rubble and cannot be recovered."

I wasn't sure if we were referring to the same location. If his book was published and identified my spot, all my efforts would be rendered meaningless. While solving the mystery on my own would be personally fulfilling, some acknowledgment would certainly be welcome.

I had reached a dead end. Here I was, holding the solution to a puzzle that had consumed others' entire lives, ready to share my findings, yet all I received was dismissal. I searched for another expert who would talk to me.

The only person willing to speak with me was Ron Feldman, a treasure hunter and renowned historian of the Lost Dutchman legend. He had dedicated decades to searching for the Lost Dutchman Mine. He believes the mine is located near Roger's Canyon, but that's because he didn't understand how crafty the map creators were. His theories aren't all wrong; Feldman also believes Abe Reid may have played a role in the death of Adolph Ruth. As it turns out, his theories have come closer to the truth than anyone else's so far. Feldman owns the OK Corral in Apache Junction, a museum focused on the Lost Dutchman mystery, where visitors can step into the Old West through horseback rides and guided tours.

This was December 2023. Anxious about San Felice's impending book, I made a final attempt by contacting Feldman. I began with an email, expressing my interest in his research about Ted Cox's account of Abe Reid carrying Adolph Ruth's body. When I followed up with a phone call, he seemed approachable and invited me to share my findings, agreeing to discuss them at the OK Corral Stables near Apache Junction. Encouraged, I promptly sent my document via Google Drive.

Then came silence; no response followed.

After several days, I called again to confirm he'd received it. During our conversation, I brought up San Felice's book. Feldman dismissed my concerns, saying, "Don't worry about Jack. He's searching in the wrong direction, far to the east."

Initially relieved, my comfort soon gave way to alarm. None of the so-called experts were even near the truth. While I believed I could reach the mine with proper planning, I had just handed Ron Feldman all my research. Now that he had the information, it would probably become public knowledge. I realized I might never reach the site before Feldman, or his sons, got there first.

In a panic, I called him again. He picked up.

"I couldn't open your attachment," he said.

"What do you mean?" I asked.

"I don't know how to use Google," he replied.

He hadn't even downloaded the document.

I told him I would resend the document and resolve the issue. It wasn't entirely truthful, but I needed to end the call quickly so I could remove the file from Google Drive before anyone downloaded it.

There I remained, clinging to my discovery, yet desperate to make progress.

As I mentioned before, this wasn't solely about uncovering treasure, though that would certainly be thrilling. More importantly, it was about solving the historical puzzle and potentially preventing further tragedies. And yes, I'll confess; I also wanted some recognition for what I'd uncovered. I am still very grateful to Ron for being willing to hear me out.

Yet he, like every other expert, is locked into his own interpretation of the clues. And why wouldn't they be? Nearly all of them have books to sell, each pointing to a different "true" location. Some are deep in the Superstitions; others are scattered across neighboring states. Even those without books still profit. The lore itself pays the bills. An unsolved mystery is far more lucrative than a solved one.

The only alternative I could see was one I'd been putting off: navigating the tedious and bureaucratic labyrinth of government agencies. A process guaranteed to test my patience and consume valuable time.

Red Tape

The one thing all the experts seem to agree on is their disdain for the process of obtaining something called a Treasure Trove Permit. They all said the same thing: "The U.S. Forest Service will never approve another Treasure Trove Permit." At first, I assumed they were exaggerating, but after hearing the same line repeated across the board, I realized many people took it as fact.

I started digging into the regulations myself. If I wanted to dig anywhere near the mine, I had to go through the U.S. Forest Service. Their website outlined the rules, and the distinction between prospecting and mining was crucial. Prospecting, which is defined as "gathering information on mineral resources," is allowed in certain areas, but only with an approved Plan of Operation. Mining, defined as "any activity that attempts to extract minerals (which are valuable and locatable) from their natural setting," has been prohibited since 1984.

Even something as simple as gold panning is regulated. If you find gold but don't extract any minerals, it's considered prospecting. But if you do extract minerals, it becomes mining. And if you're looking to uncover one of Waltz's legendary caches, that's a separate category entirely. That requires a Treasure Trove Permit.

To obtain one, you must provide evidence of treasure "of such a character that a person of ordinary prudence would be justified in the expenditure of labor and funds, with a reasonable possibility of success." The permit, if granted, would only be valid for a specific number of days, and the site would be subject to inspection.

Despite all the warnings, I decided to reach out. I contacted a local Forest Service office and was referred to a regional supervisor and a local archaeologist. We traded emails and phone calls, but in the end, I received the same answer everyone else had: "We no longer approve Treasure Trove Permits."

I thought back to all the Dutch hunters who'd shared similar experiences. Most of them gave up after that. I didn't.

Instead of walking away, I decided to escalate the matter. I wanted to understand who had the final say. Was there an appeal process? Who oversees the Forest Service? That search led me to the Senate Committee on Energy and Natural Resources, which helps draft legislation and oversees agencies like the U.S. Forest Service. And one of the members of that committee just happens to be Senator Mark Kelly, the U.S. Senator from Arizona. If anyone knew about the Lost Dutchman Mine, surely it would be him.

I found his Facebook page and clicked the "Contact Us" button, which took me to his official website. I emailed his office, explaining that I believed I had discovered the location of the Lost Dutchman Mine and that I was willing to submit a formal application for a Treasure Trove Permit. I also explained that the Forest Service had been unwilling to consider any such requests, and I asked whether he or his office could assist in urging them to reconsider.

To my surprise, Senator Kelly's team responded quickly. They expressed interest but needed me to formally apply through the Forest Service first so they could track the process.

What I was hoping for was simple. I wanted the Forest Service to review the evidence, close off the site, and send a research team to investigate. Were there Jesuit artifacts? Spanish or Mexican tools or structures? The Mexican mine I had located was just ten feet from Waltz's. What else might be buried there?

There was precedent. Ron Feldman and Bob Schoose were reportedly the last people, and possibly the only ones, to receive a Treasure Trove Permit. Both had the financial means to hire archaeologists and pay for a professional excavation team. Feldman spent five years completing the paperwork, paying fees, and conducting archaeological and cultural surveys before he was legally allowed to dig. He ultimately didn't find any treasure. Still, I figured if they had both been wrong about the mine's location, maybe they were also wrong about the Forest Service. That was years ago. Things might have changed.

In January 2024, I submitted my own permit application. I wanted everything handled properly and transparently. I wanted the site preserved. I did not want a repeat of the chaos of the 1960s, when Dutch hunters were reportedly shooting at one another in the Superstitions. And I certainly did not want an agency destroying the site, as happened with Abe Reid's dig, simply to keep others from searching.

I carefully filled out the forms, listed the team, and named the operation. I was supposed to include an archaeologist, though I wasn't sure where to find one. For equipment, I anticipated needing shovels, a metal detector, and possibly ground-penetrating radar. I made it clear I didn't want to damage the landscape or interfere with anything culturally or environmentally significant. I just wanted to dig at the site I had identified.

This was where it got complicated. The permit would only apply to defined treasure, such as gold bars or jewelry. Gold ore, still embedded in its natural rock, wouldn't count. If I found refined gold, such as cobbled gold or ingots, I believed I'd be entitled to remove it. And if the Forest Service decided to handle the excavation themselves, I hoped I'd still be allowed to claim it, since I had found the site in the first place.

I double-checked everything, made sure the application was complete, and submitted it.

Two months later, the Forest Service responded; my application was denied.

Their explanation was that the proposal "would not promote the conservation ideals of the agency." They admitted that Treasure Trove Permits are issued in rare cases, but mine did not meet their criteria because it didn't align with their mission to preserve the forest.

I didn't understand. How exactly was I violating their conservation mission? I wasn't proposing an earth-moving operation. Just a few people, maybe two, using minimal tools and technology to locate something very specific. My plan, if anything, would reduce the amount of random, destructive digging happening across the range. It would help conservation, not hinder it.

After a few days of thinking it over, I realized my application probably hadn't been strong enough. I didn't provide enough detail about the timeline, the type of equipment, mitigation of site disturbance, ecosystem protection measures, or even the estimated costs.

But beyond that, something else bothered me. The tone of the denial felt condescending. The response quoted parts of my own application out of context to highlight its shortcomings. Maybe my writing lacked polish. I had tried to keep it simple and to the point, but the tone I got back made me feel like I was being mocked.

The rejection sent me into another tailspin. Was I being paranoid about someone jumping my claim? Maybe. But if I had figured it out, someone else could too.

I considered reaching out to Senator Kelly's office again. But the idea of going through this long, bureaucratic process again made me hesitate. I remembered what Feldman and Schoose said about how drawn-out their permit process had been. Each time they applied, the Forest Service found another reason to delay it. I could have been stuck in that loop for many years. I didn't have many years.

So, I made a decision; I put the permit issue on hold.

If the authorities weren't going to help me protect the site, then maybe the only thing left was to go see it for myself. I had the maps. I had the location. Nothing was stopping me from going straight to the source.

Trial by Error

The time had come to put my theory to the test. If I was ever going to prove my theory about the mine's location, I had to get up there myself. Easier said than done. Hiking the desert mountains of Arizona is no joke. While it's a popular activity, only fools attempt it unprepared. Every year, heat exhaustion, dehydration, and falls claim lives. By April, hiking season in the Superstition Mountains is nearly over. Once the temperature hits 90 degrees, it's too dangerous. Even in the 80s, the sun makes it brutal. But there was no getting around it; I had to get my butt up there.

My first attempt was in April 2023. I knew better than to do it alone, so I brought my son Bryce and my brother-in-law Robert. None of us had been out there before. We didn't know what to bring or how to prepare. On the map, it looked like a four-mile hike. The photos made it seem easy. I couldn't have been more wrong. The terrain was unforgiving, especially for someone out of shape. We barely made it a quarter mile before I called it. I was in pain, Robert was in pain, and I knew we had to go back and rethink things.

The second attempt felt like something out of a *National Lampoon* movie. This time I brought my daughter Sage, my friend Bill, and my other brother-in-law, Scott. I warned everyone that I didn't know exactly what we were getting into. If we made it to the mine, great. If not, at least we'd have an adventure. I also reminded them to be cautious. I'd heard too many stories about people who wandered into those mountains and never came out.

From the start, things were off the rails. Scott showed up looking like Tackleberry from *Police Academy*, fully camouflaged, armed with two handguns, an AR-15, and over 250 rounds of ammo. I looked at him and said, "Jesus Christ Scott, we're not shooting up the place. There aren't any Indians or cowboys hiding behind the rocks."

Then there was Sage, who absolutely refused to camp without a bathroom. She was sixteen and made that very clear. So, I bought a portable camping toilet. I had no idea there were so many models to choose from. After some research, I picked a heavy-duty version rated for a thousand pounds. The box even had an elephant sitting on it. I figured if it was good enough for an elephant, it would handle us just fine.

We hit the trail around eight in the morning. About a mile in, we came across a locked gate near one of the ranches that border the wilderness area. That forced us to hike an extra mile just to reach our intended starting point. The road beyond that was rough. We managed maybe half a mile before slowing to a crawl. I was still out of shape, and Scott, loaded down with weapons and ammo, wasn't much better off. He fell behind.

I decided to take a break right there on the trail. Since I was lugging around that portable toilet, I figured I might as well use it as a chair. I unfolded the seat, picked a spot, and sat down. But apparently, I hadn't latched it properly. The whole thing collapsed, and I fell backward into a patch of thorns, my head pointing downhill, arms and legs flailing.

"Sage, help me up," I called out. Instead of helping, she asked for my phone and took a picture of me sprawled out on the trail, shirt hiked up, belly exposed. I was humiliated and in pain, but I couldn't stop laughing. Teenagers.

It was chaotic, slow, and nothing went as planned, but I kept going. Every mistake taught me something. Each time the mountain threw a challenge at me, I learned a little more. And I wasn't done yet.

Putting the Maps to the Test

In the weeks that followed, I returned to the mountain again and again, armed with clues from the Peralta Heart Map and satellite imagery from Google Earth. Friends and family often joined me, each trip turning into its own story filled with misadventures, minor injuries, and new frustrations. But with every hike, I was learning. I got stronger, more prepared, and more familiar with the land.

As the Forest Service warns, one of the hardest parts of a back-country trip is just finding the right trailhead. There are multiple options, but the one I had mapped led us through Queen Valley, heading north on Elephant Butte Road. The pavement eventually gave way to dirt, and the road got rough. Still, with a 4x4, it was manageable. I kept pushing forward until we reached Tortilla Canyon. From there, I parked the truck and hiked northeast for about a mile to reach Randolph Canyon.

On my third serious attempt, I brought my nephew Tyler and his friend Ethan. They were both in their early thirties, fit, upbeat, and ready for anything. I warned them the terrain would be rough and pointed to the general area of the mine, just two miles away. "No problem," they said. "We hike five miles a day. We've got plenty of water." Six hours later, I got a call over the walkie-talkie. They were turning back. They'd tried following the ravine marked on the maps, but it was hopeless. There was thick brush, massive boulders, and no clear path.

That's when it really hit me. If two fit guys couldn't get through that ravine, how had the Dutchman and his mules done it?

In early May, I came back with my cousin Kevin and his nephew Josh. This time, I was determined not to leave empty-handed. We reached the same ravine, and I knew we needed a new approach. I pulled out the Peralta Heart Map again. If the ravine was a dead end, maybe we had to go over the heart instead. We tried that, starting at the pointed end, but it didn't work either. We scouted every possible route before finally turning back, exhausted and demoralized.

I knew I was close. Too close to push forward in the summer heat, though. The temperature made it impossible to continue safely, so I paused until the season turned.

While I waited, I kept digging into the history and the clues. I reread everything I could find, trying to piece together the final steps. And that's when I remembered something important. The Dutchman had said, "If you find the mine, you can find the cache." I was confident I had found the mine. That meant the next step was finding the cache.

I went back to the simplest, most overlooked clue of all, the Dutchman's Doodle Map (Figure 70).

Figure 70- The Doodle Map. The feature often mistaken for Weaver's Needle is not a hill or mountain.

The map doesn't make it obvious. There's no "X" marking the spot. But there had to be a reason he drew it the way he did. This is when I matched the trails on the map to the terrain on Google Earth. Suddenly, it was clear as day to me. There's the looped path and the glove-shaped mountain. The path that leads to the Quarter Circle U Ranch is in the middle of the map. It is the diagonal line that stops abruptly. That's got to be the location of the cache, I thought. If you continue that line to the northeast, it also goes to the Quarter Circle U Ranch.

Waltz said he camped right above the ravine. It turned out that ravine was Randolph Canyon. There's a trail starting about 300 feet north of Randolph Canyon that heads north-northwest. It continues pretty much straight for about 500 feet. There's a flat area, about 100 feet across, right in the middle of that path. To me, it was the most obvious place to camp if I wanted to stay out of the wash and have clear visibility of any approaching trails. That had to be where he camped. Another clue was that he buried the treasure within view of his campsite. I couldn't wait to go back and test this theory.

It wasn't until September that the heat finally let up. When I went back, the first few attempts were failures. One time I wandered around with Kevin and my friend Shawn Ostapuk, but we were mostly just getting our bearings. The next time, my cousin Johnny Ray Martinez came along. True to form, I hurt myself getting out of the truck and sent him ahead with instructions. He had no clue what he was looking for and only made it about a mile in. The next attempt with Johnny and his brother Benjamin was more of the same, wasted trips. On the eighth try, three cousins joined the adventure. I was still in pain from my injury, so I rented a quad. Still, no luck.

Over the months, I pieced together clues from the stories, ran into dead ends, learned the backcountry terrain, and kept returning to the drawing board.

Back home, I reviewed my notes. I knew I had stumbled upon something connecting Travis Tumlinson to the hidden gold cache. I searched *TreasureNet,* an online forum for treasure hunters, for "cache" and "Dutchman." What I found made everything start to fall into place. The Tumlinsons and Bob Garman, the same names I'd come across researching the stone maps, were the ones who found a million dollars' worth of cobbled gold in Hewitt Canyon, about six miles south of Randolph Canyon. In the 1950s, gold was steady around $35 per troy ounce. One million dollars back then meant about 28,500 troy ounces, almost 2,000 pounds. I did the math, and that would be worth over $60 million today.

According to U.S. Army specs, a pack mule can carry between 150 and 300 pounds. Some reports say mules can haul up to 500 to 800 pounds. Transporting 2,000 pounds of gold would have required five to seven trips under normal conditions. With two mules working together, the trips could be cut in half. This made it completely plausible that Jacob Waltz could have made six trips to the mine from his camp, or fewer if he had a partner with another mule.

The treasure hunting community generally agrees that the Tumlinsons and Bob Garman found a large gold cache, though they claimed it was in a different canyon. I believe they actually uncovered the Dutchman's cache but tried to hide its true origin. Tom Kollenborn, in interviews and his book, says he and his father were with Garman and the Tumlinsons in Randolph Canyon in the 1950s while they examined the maps. At the time, he didn't grasp the significance of the location.

During my search, I found a shallow depression along the trail, about ten feet long and two or three feet deep. At first, I thought it was just natural erosion. Of course, I'll never know for sure. But remembering the Tumlinson story, I realized they found the mine before me. While disappointing, this discovery helped me focus my search. Had I not found that pit, I might still be wandering through those two rugged acres today hoping I was wrong about them finding the cache.

This also gave me a new perspective on the stone maps. Tumlinson needed to explain his sudden wealth without revealing the real discovery. By promoting the legend of ancient stone maps, he created both an explanation for his fortune and a distraction from the truth. Or maybe, as some suggest, he did it just for his own amusement.

My ninth expedition took place in January 2024. This time, my cousin Johnny, my brother-in-law Rob, and Rob's son Stephen joined me. By then, some family had lost interest, and they were the only ones I could convince to come along. Several months had passed since my last trip, and while I wasn't starting completely from scratch, I did need to reorient myself as the terrain had changed. Recent rains left the air cool and refreshing and the grass abundant. It was beautiful and inviting. I couldn't wait to start the journey.

We drove the truck until about a quarter mile short of the parking area when a tire blew out. My Excursion had aftermarket lugs, but the spline didn't fit. That meant I couldn't change the tire, even though I had a spare, a jack, and lug wrench. I was prepared for anything, except bad luck. Decision time: hike out now or push forward and deal with the tire later? I sure didn't want to become a statistic. I had no idea how long the hike would take or what we'd encounter, so I decided to hike out. It was the right call.

Luckily, I was able to move the truck off the road to let others pass. We hiked back a couple of miles toward Queen Valley and ran into some javelina hunters. Their season runs from January to March. They kindly gave Rob a ride back to his truck, and Rob came back to pick us up about a mile from Elephant Butte. It took me a week to return and fix the tire.

Into the Heart

By the tenth attempt, I had decided to give up on finding the cache. I figured it was long gone, probably discovered years ago. So, I refocused on the mine itself. This time, I wasn't about to risk taking my truck again. Instead of renting another quad, I went with a four-seater UTV that could get us as deep into Randolph Canyon as possible before we continued on foot. Sage and Bill joined me for this trip, and our target was the heart formation. We left just after sunrise with the whole day ahead of us.

We towed the UTV on a trailer along a rough dirt road until we neared Elephant Butte, not far from the CCR Ranch. From there, we transferred into the UTV and continued along the increasingly rugged trail. The UTV saved us about a mile of hiking, and it cut through the terrain with ease. It wasn't just efficient, it was actually a fun ride. We reached Randolph Canyon and made it to the middle of the heart formation by about 10:30 a.m. Across a deep ravine, I spotted a depression in the side of the mountain that I believed was the mine shaft. It was less than a mile away in a straight line, but there was no obvious way to reach it.

"There's got to be a path between here and there," I told Bill and Sage.

We decided to split up. Bill headed east toward the pointed end of the heart while Sage and I took the northern curve. The terrain was unforgiving, gullies, boulders, thorny brush, and cactus in every direction. After a couple of hours of fighting our way through, Sage and I gave up and worked our way back to the center of the heart.

Bill had better luck. He managed to cross the ravine, though it wasn't easy. Later he described jumping from boulder to boulder, dodging cactus and brush every step of the way.

By the time we regrouped around 4:00 p.m., Bill was wiped out. "This is impossible," he said. "You've got an interesting theory, but it's not working out here." And I had to admit, it was hard to argue. There was just no way an old man with a mule could have made that journey, not through that terrain.

It took us another couple of hours to get back to the UTV, then another thirty minutes of driving to return to my truck. The sun had already set. I could feel Bill's frustration. I worried I'd lost him for good on this search. But I wasn't ready to give up yet.

Early the next season, I made my eleventh attempt. I rented another UTV and left before dawn. "Today's the day," I told my three cousins. "We're going to find that mine." We oriented ourselves toward the same target and set out. But once again, we couldn't find the trail. So, we pushed forward blindly through the underbrush. Every foot forward was a fight. It took us four or five hours just to make it about 200 feet. By 2:00 p.m., we stopped to get our bearings. I wanted to reach the overlook where we could see the mine, but we had no visibility, just a general sense of direction.

I tried to keep everyone moving, but we were all scratched, bruised, and worn out from pushing through the thorns. Finally, my cousins had enough. "Let's turn back," they said.

"It's a struggle, I know," I replied. "But there has to be an easier path. There's got to be a path."

Epiphany

Every expedition into those mountains brought me a little closer to solving the puzzle. Each failed attempt ruled out another possibility and revealed a new one. On our next trip, I told my two cousins, "Today isn't about finding the mine. Let's focus only on locating the path." Once again, we came up empty. Only one section remained unexplored, the northwest side of the heart formation. I'd searched there before, but the terrain had always been too rough to cross. Still, I returned to Google Earth, determined to find something I'd missed.

This time I took a different approach. Using elevation data, I scanned the ravine for spots where the ground dropped less than a foot every five feet. That's when a line appeared on the screen, a subtle but clear path (Figure 14). It was the only stretch of gentle terrain in the entire ravine. "This could work," I thought. "This is walkable." I gathered my cousins and showed them what I found. I said, "I know it's been frustrating, but I believe I've found the path." There was some excitement, and two cousins agreed to come test it.

We packed machetes to cut through the thick brush and hiked right to the spot I found. It was almost like magic, the wilderness opened up. Beneath years of overgrowth, we uncovered a narrow but unmistakable footpath heading straight into the ravine. It led to a clearing marked by a massive, flat-topped boulder (Figure 71). This wasn't just a rock; it looked like the perfect resting place. The kind miners might have used more than a century ago. It may even match the "Ruines" shown on the old Goldmines Map (Figure 72). No structures were visible under the dense vegetation around the boulders, but the way that rock sat made it feel like a real waypoint. If there was once a settlement here, the ruins are gone. We didn't explore it much, since we were focused on reaching the mine, but the spot deserves a closer look.

Figure 71- Hidden resting spot near where it says "Ruines" on the map, courtesy of Cristian M.

Figure 72- Detail from MInas del Oro Map showing possible location of resting spot at "Ruines."

On to the Mine

Finding the path helped restore some faith in me within the family. And, as usual, word spread fast. For the fourteenth attempt, my niece Danni (32) and my cousin Josh (20) decided to join. After realizing from previous day trips that we needed more time, the goal this time was to cover as much ground as possible and camp overnight.

We made it about three-quarters of the way before nightfall, getting past the ravine and roughly halfway between it and the base of the big hill where, I believed, the mine was located.

It was late February, perfect hiking weather during the day but absolutely freezing at night. We were all worn out and chilled to the bone, and it wasn't until about 8:30 a.m. that we finally crawled out of our sleeping bags. I remember thinking, Damn, if it took us all day just to get here, that's exactly how long it's going to take to get back. I didn't think I had it in me to make it up the mountain that day.

So I said, "You know what? All I need are photos. I don't need proof of gold. You guys aren't equipped to take samples or even know what to look for. Plus, there may still be old traps up there, waiting for the next unlucky Dutch hunter. It can be dangerous. I just want you to take photos."

I gave them specific instructions: get a shot of the mine, an exterior view looking into the pit, and a few other angles that might serve as proof.

Both of them were young, fit, and game for the climb. We weren't sure if there'd be a signal that high up, so we brought walkie-talkies just in case. Despite the late start, the day was shaping up to be a good one.

But, of course, this is my family we're talking about; my niece Danni, who's a bit clumsy (a family trait), managed to lose her walkie-talkie somewhere on the trail. Thankfully, we still had 5G cell service up there, so we switched to texting.

Then, just as things were back on track, she dropped her iPhone. Gone. That was the end of her taking photos. Josh did his best, but not knowing exactly what he was supposed to document, he took a few random shots before the two of them spent the rest of their time searching for her phone, with no luck.

To make matters worse, it was a brand-new iPhone. That one stung a bit.

If at First You Don't Succeed

I just wasn't going to give up. Each attempt brought me closer to the goal, and my family's enthusiasm never seemed to fade. For my fifteenth attempt, my niece and two cousins joined me for another two-day trek. I'd walked this route plenty of times by now, but that didn't make it any easier.

Spring brought a new challenge. We don't get much rain in the desert, but when it does come, usually in February and March, the mountain transforms. What was once dry and dusty becomes a vibrant green pasture. Tall grass and thick weeds cover everything. That's the hardest part: the grass. Sometimes it's up past your knees. You know the path beneath you, but you can't see it. You're stepping on loose rocks, small boulders, sometimes cactus, and you never know if the next step will land in a hole or on a snake. All of us fell at some point, but luckily no one got hurt.

By nightfall on the first day, we'd made it about three-quarters up the hill leading to the saddle. From there, I could see the mine again, just across the ravine, almost directly opposite us. I was thrilled to make it that far, but I was also exhausted. It was too dark to press on, so we set up camp near the site I believe to be the old Spanish ruins, the same location the Dutchman may have referred to as the "Rock House" (Figure 85). I tossed and turned most of the night but finally fell into a deep sleep just before dawn.

A few hours later, we were back on our feet. We climbed up to the saddle and started to take it all in. Amazingly, we found my niece's iPhone. The one she'd dropped during a previous trip. I was able to recover the photos, but unfortunately, they turned out to be of the wrong mine, most likely the nearby Mexican mine. It's an easy mistake; there are several mines in the area, all close enough to be confused.

Still, I now had some photos I could analyze later. After snapping a few more, we began the long return. We needed to reach my parked truck before dark.

"We've got to go," my cousin said. "It took us a whole day yesterday, and another three hours today, just to get here."

"But going down is a hell of a lot easier than going up," I replied.

It didn't matter. They weren't interested in hiking after dark. And I couldn't really blame them. They were playing it safe.

As spring turned to summer, the heat became unbearable. We decided to pause the search until fall. Over the next few months, I rested, reviewed our findings, and made preparations for the next push. Originally, we planned to head out again by mid-October, but temperatures were still hovering near 100°F (38°C), far too hot for hiking rugged mountain trails. We waited two more weeks and finally set out in late October, just before Halloween, when the air was cool and dry.

For this expedition, I invited my friend Daniel Harrington to join us. Daniel, in his early thirties and in great shape, was just the kind of help I needed. My cousins Kevin and Josh couldn't make it due to other commitments, so I needed someone capable of reaching the harder spots I couldn't manage on my own.

The saddle area offered a flat section with steep ridges rising on either side (Figure 73). Its southern slope dropped off sharply just below the mine site, much steeper than the path we'd taken to reach the saddle (Figure 76). Judging it too risky for me, I stayed behind to scout the surrounding area. The saddle itself made for a great campsite and base of operations. We even found and reused an old fire ring, evidence that others had camped here long before us.

We didn't uncover anything significant on the saddle that day. If any artifacts had once existed there, time, erosion, and vegetation had likely buried them.

Daniel Harrington was able to climb up the eastern ridge (Figure 73) to investigate the mine from the top (Figure 78). The climb from the saddle is about 35 feet up, but then it drops about 60 feet down over the edge.

Figure 73- Camp on saddle, taken from Western hill, courtesy of Cristian M.

Figure 74- View from top of the saddle, facing East towards the hill with the mine

Figure 75- View from top of the saddle, facing West away from the mine

Figure 76- View of mining area from top of the saddle

Lost Dutchman Mine

Mexican Mine

Figure 77- View of the mining area from two-room cave ruins

Figure 78- View into Dutchman Mine pit and overlooking the ravine, taken from above, courtesy of Daniel H.

Figure 79- View of 18-inch quartz vein leading into Dutchman Mine pit from above, courtesy of Ethan E.

The pit mine descends about 10 feet and extends approximately 12 feet to the edge. You can clearly see the remnants of an 18-inch quartz vein running downward (Figure 79).

After capturing several good aerial photos of the mine site, we agreed to return with a rope ladder. This would allow someone to safely descend into the pit and ensure they could climb back out. The last thing we wanted was to get trapped in an abandoned mine shaft with no exit.

I organized a planning meeting at a local coffee shop called the Lost Dutchman Coffee House. The name appealed to me; if you're going to plan a meeting at a coffee shop, why not have fun with it. I invited everyone who had assisted me over the previous two years to see if they were interested in making one final attempt. Our objective was to coordinate a multi-day exploration. Ethan Eisner, my nephew's friend who had joined us on the third attempt, immediately jumped at the opportunity. He was especially excited to learn that I had already located the mine and knew the route. We scheduled the trip for the weekend of January 24 and began preparing our gear, including climbing ropes and a rope ladder.

The team successfully accessed the mine and collected several loose quartz samples from the surface, although no visible gold was found. They extended the search to the hillside above the mine entrance, photographing key features until an approaching storm forced them to cut the survey short. Before departing, we agreed to schedule a more comprehensive follow-up expedition.

For our second trip, I expanded the team to include additional family members and associates: my cousins Richard Nieto and Cristian Murillo; Cristian's son, David Chavez; and Cristian's friends Daniel Zrike and his brother, Dillon Zrike. The team took more photographs and was able to explore the area more thoroughly.

Figure 80- South-facing view of valley from saddle, showing two peaks and heart mesa centered, with Queen Valley in distance.

Figure 81- Rock face next to Lost Dutchman Mine resembling a horse head

Figure 82- Horse head rock face with Lost Dutchman Mine behind it, courtesy of Ethan E.

Figure 83- View of valley from two-room ruins, courtesy of Daniel H.

Figure 84- View of two-room cave and Spanish ruins from saddle area, mine to the left outside frame

Figure 85- View of two-room cave and Spanish ruins from near saddle

Figure 86- View of mining area from two-room cave and Spanish ruins, courtesy of Daniel H.

Figure 87- View of El Sombrero Mountain from top of saddle facing north, courtesy of Cristian M.

Figure 88- Cave behind Lost Dutchman Mine, courtesy of Cristian M.

Figure 89- View from inside cave behind the Lost Dutchman Mine, courtesy of Daniel H.

Figure 90- Cave below Lost Dutchman Mine dug by Mexican miners, courtesy of Kevin F.

Figure 91- Closeup of cave below Lost Dutchman Mine dug by Mexican miners, courtesy of Kevin F.

Into the Mine

During our initial descent into the mine, we discovered a symbol carved into the rock wall, a precise and deeply cut "V" (Figure 92). The most straightforward interpretation is that it signifies a vein of gold-bearing quartz. Prospectors often used simple but effective symbols in the field, and a "V" served as a practical shorthand for "vein," pointing out valuable mineralization. Its craftsmanship and placement suggest intentional marking rather than coincidence, making it likely that whoever carved it wished to indicate the presence of gold at that spot. This is not an isolated occurrence, as other carved "V" symbols are found throughout the Superstition Mountains, including the Iron Cross in the Bat Cave. That particular symbol is often attributed to Jesuit origins, suggesting that the "V" may carry both practical mining significance and a deeper historical connection.

The location of Lost Dutchman's Mine is latitude 33.416268° and longitude -111.283394°

Figure 92- V (or y) carved into wall, courtesy of Ethan E., and iron-cross in cave, from "Legends of the Superstition Mountains" TV show

There is compelling evidence supporting this theory. Consider the iron-cross found in a cave near this location; when paired with generations of local stories, it becomes clear why many have long suspected Jesuit involvement. Historical records show the Jesuits operated mines throughout the Americas before their expulsion in 1767. They employed native laborers and allegedly concealed some operations when pursued by the Spanish Crown. This raises the possibility that Jacob Waltz's gold might have originated from one of these abandoned Jesuit mines. At the very least, the theory aligns with known facts.

However, tangible proof remains scarce. No definitive archaeological finds or archival documents verify Jesuit activity in the Superstition Mountains. The argument depends largely on ambiguous carvings, treasure hunters' claims, and local folklore. While the Jesuits' abrupt expulsion could explain their need for secrecy, this narrative ultimately exists in a gray area between plausible history and persistent legend.

Figure 93- 18-inch quartz vein with hematite, it has been completely mined out all the way down to floor, courtesy of Cristian M.

We found the famed 18-inch-wide vein of rose quartz with hematite running through it, extending vertically approximately 12 feet into the mine floor (Figure 93). The vein shows clear evidence of mining, with worked sections ranging from less than an inch to several inches deep. For scale, we used a standard 5-gallon bucket measuring 14.5 inches tall, since we had forgotten the tape measure at home.

Figure 94- Measuring quartz vein with 14 ½ inch tall 5-gallon bucket to verify, courtesy of Cristian M.

Figure 95- 18-inch vein showing it had been mined out, courtesy of Cristian M.

Figure 96- Daniel Z. and Steve G. exploring Lost Dutchman Mine., courtesy of Cristian M.

Figure 97- Close-up of a mined-out quartz vein ranging from under ½ inch to 3 inches thick. Courtesy of Ethan E.

Figure 98- Holes in Lost Dutchman Mine walls, courtesy of Ethan E.

The walls of the mine are lined with evenly spaced holes running vertically. These may have served as anchor points for wooden beams or poles, forming part of a simple scaffolding system that allowed miners to safely climb and work the steep faces. The crescent-shaped marks along the rock suggest pick mining, where miners struck and pried the stone with hand tools, leaving behind characteristic curved fractures. Similar techniques were used well into the early 20th century, with temporary wooden structures providing access to high-grade ore veins.

To determine their true purpose, the holes' shape and spacing must be examined more closely. If they are uniform and deep, they likely held structural supports for climbing or for stabilizing ladders and platforms. If they are shallower and curved, they may instead be pickaxe marks from levering out ore. Residue inside the holes, such as wood fragments or mineral deposits, could also provide clues. Historical records of mining methods used in the region might help confirm whether such pits were typically worked with scaffolding or with direct prying tools.

Both interpretations fit the evidence. The answer likely lies in the details of the holes themselves, including their depth, wear patterns, and alignment with the mine's geology.

Figure 99- Excavation marks in Lost Dutchman Mine walls, courtesy of Ethan E.

The back walls of the mine show clear evidence of secondary excavation. Pick marks scar the rock in erratic patterns, and several shallow test pits pock the surface. I can't say definitively whether they struck gold here or if this was a desperate attempt to tunnel toward the main vein, but the intensity of the digging suggests more than casual prospecting. The angled strikes in the bedrock resemble the gouging technique favored by 19th-century miners pursuing erratic high-grade deposits.

Figure 100- Floor of Lost Dutchman Mine, courtesy of Daniel Z.

The floor of the mine is rough and littered with loose silt, scattered debris, and massive boulders. This doesn't appear accidental. If anything, it suggests someone deliberately blocked it off. Some of the old tales about the Apache returning to seal the mine may hold truth. These rocks didn't simply fall here, they were likely rolled in from above and stacked with purpose. Over time, desert winds filled the cracks with dust, gradually burying everything. This wasn't merely abandonment; it feels like a concerted effort to erase this place from existence.

Figure 101- Rear view of Lost Dutchman Mine, courtesy of Dillon Z.

The above photo shows the rear section of the mine with a vertical drop of about 6 feet down to a narrow ledge. This ledge slopes downward approximately 12 feet to another drop-off point. Below this, the shaft continues downward roughly 30 feet to lower levels. The floor throughout this area consists of accumulated dirt and large boulders.

Figure 102- Cross-section view of bottom of Lost Dutchman Mine, courtesy of Dillon Z.

Figure 103- The cavernous space beneath the boulders extends to the back of mine pit, courtesy of Dillon Z.

Putting It All Together

Many clues have been tossed around about the Lost Dutchman Mine over the years. The details often change depending on who is telling the story and when they heard it. While numerous variations exist, these are the most repeated clues attributed to the Dutchman himself, the ones treasure hunters have chased for generations.

Clue: "You could stand within twenty feet of my mine and never see it."
This is not an exaggeration. Even our team struggled with it. On their second trip, they stood just twenty feet from the entrance and still could not spot it. The terrain camouflages the mine perfectly.

Clue: "From the hill above my mine, four peaks appear as one."
This refers to Four Peaks, roughly eighteen miles due north. It can be seen from the summit just north of the mine, the one I suspect they called Sombrero Mountain. From there, the distant peaks appear to align perfectly.

Clue: "There is a trick in the trail."
The key is to avoid crossing the ravine entirely. Instead, cut across the top of Heart Mesa and follow the game trails north. It would be impossible to get a mule or horse to the mine without using this route.

Clue: "The mine sits in a north-trending canyon."
The canyon's orientation is unmistakable. Its walls run north to south, casting deep shadows for most of the day.

Clue: "Beneath the main mine lies an old Mexican tunnel, dug upward toward the vein."
We found this exact tunnel. It is a narrow cave opening, clearly dug to intercept the main vein from below.

Clue: "Climb above my mine and you will see a mountain peak to the north (or south)."
This likely refers to El Sombrero Mountain to the north or Randolph Canyon to the south, depending on the version.

Clue: "You cannot descend straight to the mine from above. First follow the ridgeline, then climb down."
This is easy to understand. From the saddle, you must climb up the east side and travel southeast along the ridge to reach the pit. Then you climb down and enter the mine.

Clue: "The Mexicans dug a second tunnel from behind."
This likely refers to the cave next to the saddle. It lies directly behind the mine.

Clue: "My mine lies near an old Spanish house on a hidden ledge."
The natural rock shelter across from the mine shows clear signs of human settlement. You can see where rock walls once stood to form two separate chambers. While the roof has collapsed over time, the remaining structure suggests it was once used as a dwelling. Its position provides a direct line of sight to the mine.

Clue: "From my mine, you can see the military trail, but from the military trail, you cannot see my mine."
You can clearly see US 60 stretching past Apache Junction toward Queen Valley. Originally an Indigenous footpath, it became a strategic route for the U.S. Army during the Apache Wars (1860s–1886).

Clue: "There is a rock 'face' on the trail to my mine."
This refers to the horse-head-shaped rock formation that protrudes prominently away from the mine.

Additional clues mention cottonwood trees and references to "First Water" or "Second Water." These are especially difficult to interpret, as cottonwoods grow near nearly every water source in the region. While there are established trails named First Water and Second Water about ten miles to the northwest, the Dutchman likely used these terms differently. He probably referred to seasonal water flows in Randolph Canyon, which lies just south of Reid's Water, or to other local springs known only to miners of his era.

The Path Forward

My team and I are applying for a Treasure Trove Permit to excavate the collapsed site and uncover what history has buried there. After years of studying maps, records, and the terrain itself, I want to be part of the team that carefully reveals what's been hidden. Not just as an observer but working alongside archaeologists to document and preserve every find. This isn't about treasure hunting; it's about peeling back the layers of time to understand what really happened here. Tribal monitors will ensure we honor the site's cultural significance, while every step follows proper archaeological protocols. Some secrets aren't meant to stay buried forever.

Critical unresolved questions needing community insight:

- What happened to the gold recovered by Garman, Tumlinson, and Leasman?

- What was their relationship with Abe Reid, and why was he excluded from their discovery?

- What was the nature of Reid's association with Keenan and Purnell?

- What else did Ted Cox witness regarding Reid and the Quarter Circle U Ranch cowboys?

- Why did Travis Tumlinson and Bob Garman create the stone maps? Was it to launder gold, or was it just for their amusement?

- What do the oral histories of local Native American tribes reveal about this mine and the surrounding area?

A heartfelt thank you to the Dutch hunting community. Your knowledge, passion, and camaraderie have been invaluable on this journey. While in the beginning, I never really considered myself a Dutch hunter, I must now admit that may have changed. It is a welcoming community filled with camaraderie and a mutual respect for nature, especially the Superstition Mountains. While we've solved the mystery and answered many questions, our work isn't done. Follow along as we explore the mine and uncover its remaining secrets at **www.FoundDutchman.com**. I'll be sharing regular updates and discoveries as the adventure continues.

ABOUT THE AUTHOR

Jason Fritsch is pursuing a doctorate in Data Analytics with advanced degrees in Computer Information Systems and Business Administration. His analytical background and experience in cybersecurity roles, from security analyst to operations manager, shaped his methodical approach to investigating the Dutchman legend.

What began as answering his daughter's question about the Superstition Mountains turned into a deep exploration of the mystery. When not researching or writing, he enjoys cooking outdoors, fishing, and family game nights, simple pleasures that ground his technical work.

Figure 104- Me (Jason Fritsch) resting after long hike up hill, sitting on the saddle next to the mine, courtesy of Steve G.

This is also me...

Figure 105- Me (Jason Fritsch) just after a fall, courtesy of Sage B.

www.ingramcontent.com/pod-product-compliance
Lightning Source LLC
Chambersburg PA
CBRC090843120626
46551CB00009B/743

9 798999 867828